MARIO MOLTENI

The Clay Modelling Handbook

Learning from the Masters

Clarkson Potter/Publishers

New York

Published by Clarkson N. Potter, Inc., 201 East 50th Street,
New York, New York, 10022,
member of the Crown Publishing Group

Originally published in Italy in 1989 by Gruppo Editoriale Fabbri
S.p.A., Milan
Copyright © 1989 by Gruppo Editoriale Fabbri, Bompiani,
Sonzogno, Etas, S.p.A., Milan. English translation © 1992 by
Gruppo Editoriale Fabbri, S.p.A., Milan
Translated by Kerry Milis Parker
Layout: Ettore Maiotti

Those works not otherwise cited are those of Mario Molteni

Photo credits:
Gruppo Editoriale Fabbri Archives, Milan
(Piero Baguzzi, Alberto Bertoldi, Mario Matteucci).
Mario Molteni's sculpture was photographed
by Piero Baguzzi and Alberto Bertoldi.

Front cover illustration:
Female bust with fawn from Ibiza (V-IV century BC),
Phoenician Art. 26,5 cm. Terracotta.
Barcelona, Museo Arqueológico (detail).
Photo by Piero Baguzzi.

© SIAE, Rome, 1992 for the work by Pablo Picasso.

CLARKSON N. POTTER, POTTER and colophon are
trademarks of Clarkson N. Potter, Inc.

Printed in Italy by Gruppo Editoriale Fabbri, S.p.A., Milan

Library of Congress Cataloging-in-Publication Data

Molteni, Mario.
The clay modelling handbook: learning from the masters /
    Mario Molteni.
       p.   cm.
ISBN 0-517-58598-7: $ 15.00
1. Modelling–Handbooks, manuals, etc. I. Title.
NB1180.M65   1992   91-32937
731.4'3–dc20   CIP

ISBN: 0-517-58598-7
10 9 8 7 6 5 4 3 2 1

First American Edition

CONTENTS

A SMALL PRACTICAL GUIDE: HOW TO USE IT

Before we begin to talk about how to work with clay, there is one very important thing that I would like to say. I should like to make clear what I hope this guide will be and how you can best use it. In this way, you will know not only what you can expect from it, but also what it will not attempt to do. To put it very simply, in the short "conversations" that follow I will teach you the methods and techniques of working with clay. What I cannot do, however, is turn you into an artist.

Therefore, my discussions will not be about aesthetics or style, nor will they provide you with suggestions for projects nor describe methods of expression. In fact I will not be commenting on the artistic value of your work in any way. I do not believe it would be correct or, for that matter, even useful for me to do so. In fact, quite frankly, I do not think it is possible to develop artistic ability or reveal talent in a book such as this one which merely tries to be a useful and thorough technical aid. Such a limitation, however, should not make it any less valuable. My original aim, when I first thought about writing this book, was to provide a clear, schematic and practical guide that would teach people the correct way to work with a simple yet extremely expressive material rich with possibilities, namely, clay. This brief summary of information and technical advice, then, is meant to lead you successfully stage by stage, from beginning (when we will learn the basics) to end (when we will look at firing and how to add colour). It has been conceived expressly for those who want to work with clay and learn more about sculpture, but do not quite know how to get started, that is, what materials and tools they will need and how to use them and what methods they need to learn in order to get the results they want.

At this point I think it may be useful to clarify a few concepts before you begin to get organised. These ideas should prove useful, at least in my experience, not only as you work through this little guide, but later when you are actually working with the clay itself. Here I will be using sculpture as my example, but in fact what I have to say holds true for any artistic discipline, because the way one learns a discipline and gets to the heart of it is always the same.

Fundamentally sculpture, like painting, poetry or music, is a language and that is how I shall be treating it right from the beginning. Language is expression and it can be shaped in many different ways without necessarily changing its substance. One can express the same thing verbally, figuratively, musically or with clay: they are all legitimate modes of expression.

To shape something, to speak, write, paint, or compose a piece of music, all are different ways of bringing an idea to life. No matter what method or material is used, the intention is always the same: to express an idea, something that before only existed within us, that we want to bring out and make concrete, to expose to the light, to share. And it is through language that we communicate these ideas. But what do we mean when we say we communicate, we give life and reality to something (whether it be an emotion, a situation, a story, or an ideal) through the form and structure of language? What we are trying to say, I think, is that through language we can bring into existence and give shape to something real and concrete, something almost tangible, which previously did not exist except as an abstract and unformulated idea. The act of creating something, however, is neither automatic nor spontaneous. It is something that must be learned and this learning is acquired in specific stages. For example, in order to speak, we must first master sounds and the most basic elements of language. Then as we move on to reading and writing, we must learn the alphabet and the sounds and shapes of the letters that make it up. After that we can begin to put these letters together in more complicated units, namely words, and then put the words together to form even more complex units, that is, sentences, paragraphs and entire discourses. At the same time, while we are learning all of this, we must learn how to think logically and to understand the structure of the language, so that our words make sense and express our thoughts in a comprehensible way. This is where grammar, with all its rules, comes in. Rules and a structure are what organise and make language possible. This holds true for other kinds of language as well. Therefore, it is essential to know not only the elements of a language but also the basic rules that govern its functioning. It would be impossible to give shape to anything comprehensible and sensible if we did not respect the structure and inner logic of the language which we were going to use. That is why it is so important to begin by providing ourselves with a solid "grammatical" base before we begin to "speak" through images and shapes. Such notions, especially at the beginning, may seem boring, even discouraging, but they are not meant to dampen your enthusiasm. What I really want to do is to get you started on the right foot from the very beginning. With an intelligent start, although it may seem a bit more demanding than anticipated, you will discover you have endless possibilities opening up as you gain in experience.

Let us go back now for a moment to verbal language, with which we are most familiar. When we know a language well, and are able to speak it and write it, we eventually find we no longer need to refer constantly to the rules of grammar and syntax. Yet we still use them. It is only that with time, they become natural and spontaneous, settling into the backs of our minds. Of course, they are still around, giving structure and shape to our words. Now, however, they are extracted from our sub-conscious through our powers of logic and we no longer notice them.

As you work with clay, a similar process should take place. Once you develop a solid foundation and learn the few but fundamental rules that will be illustrated in this book, and take care to apply them rigorously and coherently, you will acquire a basic level of competence. This can then be developed so that with experience it will bear fruit. Your goal should be to arrive at a deep understanding of your subject, to master the material and make it your own, so that you can transform it in such a way that it expresses what you want. And in order to express what you want in the way that you want, you must gain total control over what you do.

Artistic expression, however, is not a purely intellectual exercise. One of the most important aspects of all artistic expression is the physical labour involved in carrying out the work. Of course, the importance of manual work should not be exaggerated but it is nevertheless indispensable that you become competent in that aspect of the work. Thanks to such competence you will avoid both embarrassment and frustration as you begin to work with this new material. This is important for it is a medium which, if you do not understand it properly or know how to work with it, can work against you, presenting you with insurmountable obstacles.

Thus we come to the importance of developing skills. This is something that can only be done with practice and experience, by actually working with the material, by getting your hands dirty, so to speak. However, this alone is not enough. You must also learn to connect your experience to the discipline of a method and direct it, by using the basic rules that you have learned, the so-called "grammar" we discussed above. In this way the "hands-on" experience becomes another part of your development, giving you more freedom and helping you to understand what you are doing in a very concrete way. This is how you will eventually become master of your actions.

In order to avoid ending up like the person who wants desperately to say something, but cannot find the words, no matter how hard he tries, you must develop your skills. They are what make the difference---what you say, its value and its beauty will depend on them, and no guide book, no matter how good, can offer you more. But it is also important to realise that skill and technical ability alone, even when very refined, cannot turn you into an artist. They can only provide you with the tools for becoming one, though after all, that is not insignificant. Talent cannot be taught and to pretend to be able to teach it would be not only incorrect but also misleading. In the course of our "conversations" then, you will learn the technical rules along with how to use tools and the methods and ways of working with clay. You will learn how to model, but not what to model or even why you should attempt it. Neither creativity nor motivation can be taught nor can they be imposed from outside. They lie within each of us, to different degrees and in different forms, and they must be respected and set free so that they can be expressed in the way and for the reasons they decide.

Now that this is clear, we can move on to the real subject of interest, keeping in mind that though there are few rules and few tools necessary, they are of fundamental importance. Therefore it would be wise to apply the former rigorously and to learn the correct way to use the latter. When you truly possess them and can use them at the right moment effortlessly and without thinking, to greater and greater effect, you will be free to do with them what you want, the language you employ to express yourself in clay.

A LITTLE BIT OF HISTORY

Sometimes when I let my imagination roam free, I try to imagine the first person to use clay. I like to think that this first person was a young child back in prehistoric times.

Each of us has had the experience in childhood of playing in the mud, enjoying the sheer sensual pleasure of thrusting our hands deep into damp earth or some other material like it, with no particular goal in mind. We did not do it thinking of anything special, we simply enjoyed the purely tactile sensation of having wet mud in our hands, the joy of manipulating a soft, malleable material, of poking our fingers into a thick squishy mass, and constantly changing its shape or progressively shaping it into forms.

We have all had the urge at one time or another to stick our fingers into the mud or in a bit of bread dough or wet plaster, in short, into anything that could be squashed or smeared or shaped with no particular idea of why we wanted to do this. When we did this, we were simply following an impulse to experience something pleasant and stimulating to the touch, to leave our imprint on the material, to feel constantly changing shapes in our hands. This impulse, spontaneous and instinctive, can become a kind of game, and it must have been something akin to this that our young ancestor experienced, playing in the mud thousands of years ago, as he discovered the possibility of creating an infinite number of different objects.

Water and earth are two of the primary elements

Bas-relief in clay from the Ivory Coast.

which have always been linked closely to human life. They are probably also the components of the first substances manipulated and worked by those strange and wonderful early human species, our ancestors. They, like us, felt that healthy and never-ending desire to play, an urge we tend to keep more or less hidden inside us most of the time, but which luckily for us, remains with us, even when we are no longer children, or even in fact, young.

This urge, or better, this inexhaustable desire to play, was one that characterised this new species of perpetually curious and eager animals, always a bit childlike at heart, who were ever ready to go and explore and do, to discover new things, and to experiment.

At first, playing with mud or clay must have been simply one more pastime but at some point early humans must have become aware that they could do more with it than simply amuse themselves: they discovered its practical value. This discovery was so important that in many ways it changed the habits, even the very lives of people for thousands of years to come.

The first objects made from clay were objects

Terracotta head, *Ife, Nigeria (XIII-XIV century), 21 cm. Nigerian Museums.*

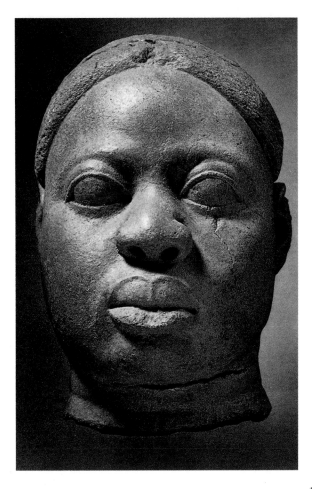

meant for everyday use: bowls, crude pots and containers of various sorts. In the beginning they were simply left out in the sun to dry. Later, however, they were dried in primitive ovens. Lightweight, easy to carry, poor conductors of heat and thus useful for keeping their contents at a constant temperature, these objects were clearly of great practical value.

The raw material used to make them was easy to find and relatively easy to work with, but its importance was not limited to that. Because of its malleability, clay could take on an inexhaustible variety of shapes, limited only by one's imagination.

Soon these objects of terracotta were valued not only for their usefulness, but also for their design and beauty. The early plain and simple objects became over time more and more refined and decorated. Their designs were engraved, given relief and painted in bright colours. To their practical value, a purely aesthetic element was added. The objects were made into decorations and furnishings, valuable as property, and as such, they also became valuable for exchange.

Distinctive shapes and designs emerged that could

Terracotta head, *Ife, Nigeria (XII-XV century), c. 29 cm. Nigerian Museums.*

Furnishings from a tomb including a Minoan glass and Egyptian objects, *Abydus, (XIX century BC). Oxford, Ashmolean Museum.*

Matrix and stamp with the god Bes struggling with a bull, *from Kythrea (VII century BC), 6 x 10 cm. Terracotta. Nicosia, Cyprus Museum.*

Round stamp with two ibises, *from Carthage (VI-V century BC), 10.8 cm diam. Terracotta. Carthage, Carthage Museum.*

13

be distinguished from each other according to their geographic and ethnic backgrounds, so that specific designs and shapes characterised and were immediately recognisable as coming from a particular place (see pictures on pages 9 to 11). Some also carried certain social connotations with them. In short, there began to be "trademarks", recognised styles. The different styles gave birth to new forms and techniques. Terracotta began to be used for all kinds of things, ranging from religious or votive objects to those that were purely artistic or decorative.

Let us now take a brief look at the history of terracotta and clay objects by tracing their development throughout the course of civilization.

The first objects made of terracotta, appearing around the fifth or sixth century BC in the East were rings of clay placed one on top of the other and then pressed together by hand. These were followed by tablets of clay compressed into a mould or shaped by pouring very watery clay into a hollowed-out form. By the end of the Neolithic period, the lathe had been invented. Initially, objects were shaped by hand with the help, per-haps, of a wooden stick, but gradually, thanks to the use of moulds, it was possible to make many copies of figures both in the round and in relief, as well as individual pieces of large sculptures which could then be assembled into a single unit.

Frequently a mould was used to shape the front of a figure, while the back would be finished by hand. This was also true of sculptural details which might be moulded separately and then put together just before the object was fired.

The earliest small terracotta figures were solid, but later hollow figures began to appear in Archaic Greece (8th-4th century BC). Both small figures and relief were painted with bright colours which were applied after firing over a coating of whitewash, used as a support.

In ancient Egypt terracotta was rarely used; the Egyptians preferred instead objects made of their own particular version of faience. It was only under the influence of Hellenistic culture that sculpture in clay became common.

On the other hand, in the region around Mesopotamia, clay was employed to make diverse objects: sarcophogi, furniture, figures and relief. Terracotta was widely used in the Minoan and Mycenaean civilisations where, even though glazed earthenware was preferred, clay was used to make small idols, animal figures, vases and sarcophogi.

Rhyton in the shape of a cart pulled by oxen, sub-Minoan art, Karfi (1200-1000 BC), h 50 cm. Terracotta. Hiraklion Museum.

Mother-goddess, seated with infant on her knees. *Cretan-Mycenaean Art, Musée du Louvre.*

On the isle of Cyprus, halfway between the Greek coast and that of Asia Minor, there developed at the end of the fourth millenium BC, a curious mix of a civilisation linked to Syria and Anatolia but influenced nevertheless by both Crete and later Mycenae.

In the time between the Neolithic and Bronze Ages an important civilisation developed on the Cyclades Islands with Crete as its most important city. Between 2600 and 1400 BC, it grew into the centre of the huge and extremely refined Minoan civilisation. Its influence spread as far as Asia Minor, Troy, Cyprus and Tirinth in the Peloponnesians, and especially to Mycenae. Mycenae later became the seat of a new culture, arising from the mixing of the indigenous population with the Achaeans, a barbarian tribe descending south from the area of the Danube. Terracotta was used often in Crete for making objects of rare beauty and elegance, which were then decorated with naturalistic motifs of an unequaled stylistic and chromatic freshness and elegance. This naturalism began to grow more stylised under the influence of the Mycenaeans and gradually transformed typical Minoan decorative motifs into designs with a more abstract and geometric character.

Idols in terracotta *from Cyprus (2nd millenium BC). Cretan-Mycenaean Art, Hannover, Kestner Museum.*

The Phoenicians came from the lands that are now called Lebanon, in particular such centres as Tyre and Byblos. There they were already a flourishing and advanced civilisation by the second millenium BC, enjoying a close rapport with the Egyptians and the Cypriots.

The Phoenicians were above all navigators and traders and between the second and throughout the first millenium BC they spread their culture and traded their goods all over the Mediterranean basin.

Like the Greeks, the Phoenicians managed to establish a phenomenal number of colonies throughout the Mediterranean world, from Asia Minor to the northwest coasts of Africa and Spain, from southern France and south central Italy to the Balearic Islands, Cyprus, and Malta. The list of their cities in the ancient world is extraordinary.

Plaquette depicting scene of adoration (V century BC), Phoenician Art, 13.5 x 8 cm. Terracotta. Paris, Musée du Louvre.

One such city was Carthage on the north coast of Africa which grew into an empire that dominated the entire Mediterranean until it was finally conquered by the Romans and destroyed.
There remain a very large number of Phoenician objects in terracotta which are testimony to the long use by the Phoenicians of this material, which was extremely malleable, economical and practically inexhaustible.
The objects are usually of a small size which, according to the zone and the period from which they came, show traces of the influence of some of the great civilizations (the Egyptians, Persians, Greeks and Cypriots) with whom the Phoenicians maintained close trade and cultural relations.
The small statues are usually painted in one or two colours and shaped or turned with some parts modelled separately and added after firing.
Small idols, very finely decorated female figures, plaques in relief, prints and moulds have all been found.
Other objects typically made of terracotta were different kinds of masks and protomes whose use was linked especially to rituals connected with death and burial, as well as occasionally for religious rituals or other uses.

Statuette of enthroned deity *from Meniko (VI century BC), Phoenician Art, 18.5 cm. Painted terracotta. Nicosia, Cyprus Museum.*

(Opposite)

Far left:
Bell-shaped votive statuette of a woman
with child, *from Bithia (III-I century BC),*
Phoenician Art, h 17 cm. Terracotta.
Cagliari, Museo Archeologico Nazionale.

Left:
Bell-shaped votive statuette with hands
covering eyes, *from Bithia*
(III-I century BC), Phoenician Art,
h 20.5 cm. Terracotta.
Cagliari, Museo Archeologico Nazionale.

Right:
Statuette of armed horseman,
from Byblos (VIII-VI century BC),
Phoenician Art, 35.5 x 24 cm.
Terracotta. Brussels, Musées Royaux
d'Art et d'Histoire.

Female bust with fawn *from
Ibiza (5th-4th century BC),
Phoenician Art, 26.5 cm.
Terracotta. Barcelona, Museo
Arqueológico.*

Male mask *from the necropolis at Akhziv, (7th-6th century BC),*
Phoenician Art, painted terracotta. Jerusalem, Israel Department
of Antiquity Museum.

Statue of a woman *(art from Canosa, Magna Graecia).*
Terracotta. Naples, Museo Nazionale.

24

Left:
Head of sphinx, *fragment of sculpture from a pediment, Thebes, temple of Apollo Ismen (?), Corinthian art (540-530 BC), h 20 cm. Terracotta. Paris, Musée du Louvre.*

Right:
Votary panel with Hades and Persephone on throne, *art from Magna Graecia, Locri (470-460 BC), h 27 cm. Terracotta. Reggio Calabria, Museo Nazionale.*

The origins of the Etruscans have always been uncertain, even in the time of the ancient Greeks and Romans. According to the Greek historian Herodotus, writing in the fifth century BC, they came from Lydia in western Asia Minor, while other chronicles of the time identified them as a people who had reached the Italian peninsula from the forests of central Europe in search of warmer climates and better lands. Dionysius of Halicarnassus, a Greek historian of the first century BC, believed that the Etruscans were an indigenous Italian race, and gave them the name Rasenna.

Possibly the descendants of the ancient Villanoviani, this refined and advanced civilisation developed between the eighth and first century BC,

Couple, *Sarcophagus from Cerveteri (Etruscan Art), terracotta. Opposite: Detail of the hands.*

along the rivers Arno and Tevere first, then up to the river Po and on to Campania at the height of their expansion.

The refinement of Etruscan art was due less to the Etruscans' mythical and obscure origins than to their frequent contact with the Greeks and Phoenicians who dominated the Mediterranean basin.

Terracotta was widely used not only for vessels and for small decorative objects, but also for large statues. Many statues from the temple of Minerva of Veio are now on display in the Museum of Villa Giulia in Rome.

These large, richly-coloured sculptures decorated the pediments of the temple, and can almost certainly be attributed to the sculptor Vulca, who worked between 510 and 490 BC. The founder of a famous school, he is the only artist from that civilisation whose name we know today and whose work we can identify with any degree of certainty. One of the most representative and popular works of Etruscan art today (also in the Villa Giulia Museum), is the sarcophagus showing a reclining couple in terracotta brought from Cerveteri and made sometime between 530-520 BC.

A very large sculpture, it was made up of individual pieces that were fired separately and then assembled.

In Archaic Greece, work with clay was widely developed, giving rise to important pottery centres like Corinth and Argolis. Examples of this work can be found in the decorative elements of the temples which were made of polychromatic terracotta. But it was among the Etruscans especially that the use and tradition became widespread, thanks in part to the influence of the high-quality work of the Greek craftsmen. The most important workshops located in Veio were mentioned also in Rome in the fifth century BC.

Decorative detailing in temples was often modelled in terracotta, as were large sarcophagi, figures and portraits.

In fifteenth century Italy terracotta came into its own, both as architectural ornamentation (reliefs, fretwork, friezes) especially in northern Italy (used by Filarete in the Ospedale Maggiore, Milan) and as an integral part of sculpture: in Emilia, for example, it was used by such famous sculptors as Niccolò dell'Arca (Pietà, Santa Maria della Vita, Bologna) and G. Mazzoni (Nativity, The Duomo in Modena) and in Tuscany by such artists as A. Rossellino, Donatello (the bust of Niccolò by Uzzano, Florence, Museo Nazionale), Pollaiuolo (Bust of Unknown Man, Florence, Museo Nazionale), Desiderio da Settignano (tondi in the Pazzi Chapel) and by the famous Della Robbia family, first by Luca who worked with glazed tondi, that is, tondi covered with tin-glazed enamel, to great effect.

Head of a man, *from Tarquinia, Central Italy (II-I century BC), Etruscan Art, h 23 cm. Terracotta. Tarquinia, Museo Nazionale.*

In Magna Grecia (Southern Italy in ancient times, where many colonies were founded by inhabitants of Greek Cities) and in Sicily, terracotta was widely used in architecture, as well as for making busts of gods and goddesses, statues, funerary urns and reliefs. During the Hellenistic period (3rd-1st century BC), there was a vast production of small clay statues throughout the Mediterranean basin that were copied from large statues, from important contemporary centres like Tanagra, Mirina (Greece), Alexandria in Egypt, Locris, Taranto, Paestum and Capua (in Italy).

In the Roman republic (6th-1st century BC) terracotta was used for making architectural details, votive statues and figurative reliefs.

Andrea Della Robbia (Florence, 1435-1525), was the nephew and partner of Luca. He was strongly influenced in his early years by the work of his uncle with whom he collaborated closely in the production of glazed ceramics in a style that also reflects the influence of Verrocchio. The frenetic activity of Andrea, the result of an ever increasing demand for his work, eventually produced a decline in its quality, giving rise to a progressive formal degeneration. Nevertheless Andrea enjoyed enormous popularity which seems merited when one looks at some of his best and most pleasing work, such as the Foundling Children ten tondi on the face of the Ospedale degli Innocenti (1463, Florence), the altar-piece of the Verna (Arezzo) with its theme of stories from the life of Christ, and the lunette of The Meeting of St. Francis and St. Dominic (1490-95, Florence, the loggia of the Ospedale di San Paolo).

Andrea Della Robbia (1435-1525): Bust of a child. *Glazed terracotta. Florence, Museo Nazionale del Bargello.*

Michelangelo Buonarroti (1475-1564): Hercules and Cacus, *h 41 cm. Terracotta. Florence, Casa Buonarroti*

Michelangelo Buonarroti, painter, sculptor, architect and poet, joined Domenico Ghirlandaio's workshop in 1488 when he had just turned 13. From 1490 to 1492 he worked for Lorenzo de'Medici and in 1496 he made his first trip to Rome. In 1498 he was commissioned to do a Pietà *for St Peter's. He returned to Florence in 1501 where the works department of the Duomo asked him to do a sculpture of David, a project he worked on for three years and which established his reputation. In 1505 Pope Julius II Della Rovere commissioned him to design his tomb which would be placed in the Church of San Pietro in Vincoli, a monumental project to be made up of 40 statues. When it was finally installed in St. Peter's in Rome, however, it consisted of only three figures (1542). From 1508 to 1512 the artist was entirely taken up with painting the frescoes for the ceiling of the Sistine Chapel. He sculpted his figure of* Moses *in 1513 and in successive years the four* Slaves *(Paris, Musée du Louvre). From 1520 to 1534 he spent his time designing the Medici tombs for the New Sacristy of the Church of San Lorenzo in Florence, with interruptions in 1528 for work on the monumental* Hercules and Cacus *(finished by Bandinelli in 1534. The study in clay reproduced here may be a first draft) and in 1529 for the building of fortifications for Florence. He returned to Rome in 1533 and from 1534 to 1541 he worked on the frescoes of* The Last Judgement *for the Sistine Chapel. In 1550 he sculpted the* Pietà *which is now on display in the Duomo in Florence and the* Rondanini Pietà *in Milan.*

Giuseppe Sanmartino (1720-1793): Figures for a nativity scene (detail), *h 25 cm. Polychromatic terracotta and cloth. Naples, Museo Nazionale di San Martino.*

Giuseppe Sanmartino, a Neopolitan sculptor, was best known for his marble Christ Lying under the Shroud *finished in 1753 (Naples, Cappella Sansevero). He worked with marble, stucco and terracotta and his work modelling nativity scene figures like those reproduced on the opposite page, was remarkable.*

31

32

Antonio Canova (1757-1822):
Eros and Psyche *(c. 1787),*
h 16 cm. Terracotta.
Possagno, Gipsoteca
Canoviana.

The sculptor Antonio Canova
spent his formative years in
Venice, moving to Rome in
1781 where he completed two
funerary monuments, one for
Clement XIV in 1787 and one
for Clement XIII in 1792.
During the Napoleonic period
he did several portraits of the
Emperor and members of his
family (Paolina Bonaparte
Borghese as Conquering
Venus *in 1808). He also did*
various other funerary
monuments, one of which was
that of Maria Cristina of
Austria (1798-1805) and
many mythological subjects,
among them the various
versions of Hebe, The Three
Graces, *and* Eros and
Psyche.

Right:
August Rodin (1840-1917):
Small study of a head,
h 11 cm. Terracotta.

Auguste Rodin, a French sculptor, studied at a special school for drawing and mathematics after being refused admittance to the Ecole des Beaux Arts. In 1864 he joined the studio of the famous sculptor Carrier Belleuse with whom beginning in 1870 he collaborated for many years on works for the decoration of the Stock Market in Brussels. In 1875 he travelled to Italy where he discovered Michelangelo and his work. In 1877, still an unknown, he sent his first important work, The Age of Bronze, to the Paris Salon. From 1879 to 1882 he worked on ceramics for manufacturers in Sevres. In 1880 the French Government entrusted him with the execution of a monumental door which Rodin called The Gates of Hell for the Musée des Arts Decoratifs in Paris which unfortunately he never finished. With the Paris Salon of 1900, when he exhibited his sculpture Man Walking, the name of Rodin became known world-wide. Among his best-known works are The Thinker (1881), The Kiss (1886), The Hand of God (1897), and The Cathedral (1908). Among his official commissions were The Burghers of Calais (1884-1895), Monument to Victor Hugo (1893) and Monument to Balzac (1892-1897).

Auguste Rodin: Female Torso I. Terracotta. Paris, Musée Rodin.

During the Middle Ages, however, the use of terracotta was almost completely abandoned until the beginning of the Romanesque era and the Gothic era when clay was once more used for decoration and the adornment of buildings, particularly churches. This usage was widely developed during the fifteenth century, especially in Lombardy and Emilia in Italy. Terracotta, as a medium in the development of large works, was also used during the Gothic period in northern Europe. It made its appearance in Italy in the fourteenth century principally in the shape of polychromatic figures. Important sculptors like Donatello used it extensively in Tuscany, while others like Nicolò dell'Arca and Luca della Robbia worked with it in northern Italy.

In more recent times, clay was used as an aid in making "sketches" (or "maquettes") and working models of projects which were then carried out in marble and bronze. Today clay has again come into its own and is being used for the final versions of sculptures as well as working models (by artists like Fontana, Fabbri, Leoncillo, Melotti).

Auguste Rodin: Draft for The Gates of Hell *(1880), h 105 cm.* Terracotta.

Aristide Maillol (1861-1944): Standing Figure of Girl Combing Her Hair *(1919/20). Terracotta.*

Aristide Maillol, a French sculptor, began his studies as a painter at the Ecole des Beaux-Arts in Paris. Then towards the end of the nineteenth century, he turned his attention to sculpture with a special interest in the female nude. Among his works were Night *(1910),* Monument to Cezanne, The Mediterranean, Pomona, Ile de France, *a series of Venuses,* Seated Nude, *and* Three Nymphs, *carried out between 1912 and 1925, and* The River *(1939-1942).*

Right:
Lucio Fontana (1899-1968): Figure at the Window *(1931). Painted terracotta. Milan, Collezione Pollini.*

Lucio Fontana: Black Figures *(1931). Painted terracotta. Milan, Collezione Fontana.*

Lucio Fontana, a sculptor and painter of Italian and Argentinian descent, finished his studies in Italy and then in 1922 returned to Argentina where he began his artistic career. He later went back to Italy where he attended the Accademia di Brera, studying with the sculptor Adolfo Wildt. During the Thirties, besides carrying out works in terracotta, like those reproduced here, he began to develop an interest in the abstract movement and became involved in the experimental work of a group of artists whose centre was the Galleria del Milione in Milan. During the Second World War, he lived in Argentina and there in 1946 he drew up the White Manifesto, *in which he laid the theoretical groundwork for spacialism, a concept which he would develop more fully after 1947 in Milan, Italy.*

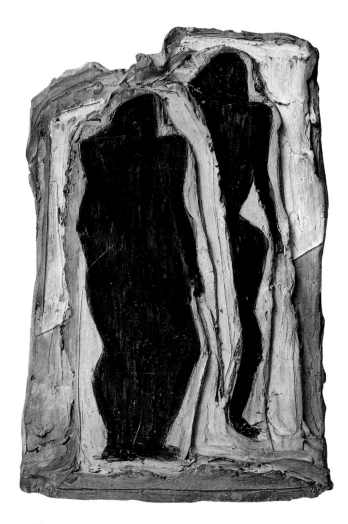

Left: Marino Marini (1901-1980): Quadriga *(1943). Terracotta. Basel, Kunstmuseum.*

Marino Marini, painter, engraver and sculptor, began to sculpt in 1929 and one of his first works was The People, *in terracotta. In 1935 he achieved his first serious recognition at the II Roman Quadriennale. When war broake out he moved to Switzerland and moved back to Milan only after it was over. In 1950 he had his first exhibition in the United States and in 1952 he won the Grand Prize for Sculpture at the Biennale of Venice. In the fifties, his artistic production reached its peak. His sculptures were bought by museums and by some of the most important private collections in Europe and around the world. Among his works are* Ersilia *(1930-49),* The Juggler *(1938)* Pomona *(1941)* The Dancer *(1949),* The Cavalier *(1949-50),* Acrobats and Jugglers *(1953-54) and* Miracle *(1955).*

Right: Arturo Martini (1889-1947): Moonlight *(1931), h 200 cm. Terracotta. Anversa, Middelheim Open Air Museum of Sculpture.*

Arturo Martini, sculptor, worked in ceramics factories from the time he was a boy, an important experience that left him with a love for the medium. In 1909, he travelled frequently to Munich to visit the studio of the sculptor Hildebrand. In 1912, he made a trip to Paris where he came into contact with Boccioni and Modigliani. In 1920, he had his first exhibition in Milan with an introduction by Carlo Carra. In 1925 he was given a room at the Biennale in Rome and the next year he had his first exhibition at the Biennale in Venice. At the Venetian Biennale of 1932 he exhibited five works in terracotta, among them, Moonlight, *right. At the 1942 Biennale he showed his famous sculpture* Girl Swimming *in Carrara marble. Among his other works are* Woman from Pisa *(1928-29),* The Shepherd *(1930), and* The Dream *(1931).*

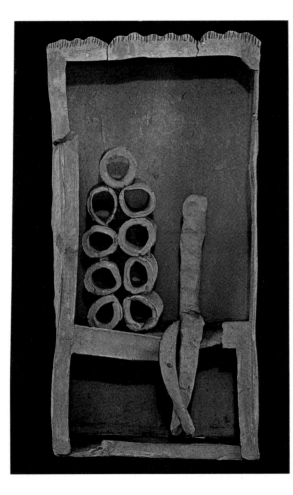

Fausto Melotti (1901-1986): Alone with Circles *(1944). Terracotta. Milan, Melotti Collection.*

Fausto Melotti, sculptor, trained first as an electrical engineer, but then decided to become a sculptor and attended classes taught by Adolfo Wildt at the Accademia di Brera. His first efforts were focused on studies of the use of space and its limitations and expression which quickly took him out of the artistic mainstream in Italy. He then developed a working rapport with non-figurative artists who tended to gravitate around the Galleria del Milione in Milan. There at their first exhibition in 1935 he showed eighteen sculptures in gesso, clay and enameled metal. In 1943, the destruction of his studio with a large portion of his work marked the beginning of a difficult period during which Melotti was forced to earn a living making ceramics. His artistic explorations during the last part of his life seemed to take two directions, one represented by stainless steel structures, often inspired by the world of music, and the other by his series of Puppet-shows *in coloured terracotta (an idea he had had as early as 1932), as well as in other material.*

Pablo Picasso (1881-1973): Owl *(1950-51), 34 x 35 x 22 cm. Painted ceramic. Marina Picasso Collection.*

The Spanish painter and sculptor Pablo Picasso carried out his artistic studies in Spain from 1900-1904 and then made four trips to Paris before he decided to move there once and for all. He very quickly established a large circle of friends in the French capital and his studio became the focal point for such young artists and writers as Jacob, Jarry, Salmon, and Apollinaire. As he was developing his skills as a painter, he also grew more interested in sculpture. In 1906-07, he began to work on Les Demoiselles d'Avignon; *during those years the cubist movement matured and Picasso became its leader and promoter. From 1930 on, he continually turned to sculpture and between 1932 and 1933 he created a series of masterpieces. In 1936 he is named director of the Prado Museum in Madrid; in 1937 he painted* Guernica. *In the years that followed up to 1945 his work as a painter and sculptor were primarily taken up with the horrors of war. Meanwhile he continued to work enthusiastically with ceramics and lithography. After an intense period of participation in the international political world (especially around 1948-50), he moved to Antibes where his desire to experiment with different materials led him to work with terracotta and ceramics. From 1961 he lived a life of retirement in his many residences, from the villa La Californie in Cannes to his castles in Vauvenargues and Mougins.*

Agenore Fabbri (born 1911); The Dog of War *(1952). Polychromatic terracotta. Milan, Private Collection.*

The sculptor Agenore Fabbri carried out his artistic studies in Pistoia and Florence and then in 1935 he moved to Albisola in Liguria. There he worked as a modeller in a ceramics factory. After the war, he did a series of figures (especially wounded animals) modelled with dramatic realism. Among his many works: The Death of a Partisan *(1952),* Motherhood *(1953), and* Man from Hiroshima *(1964).*

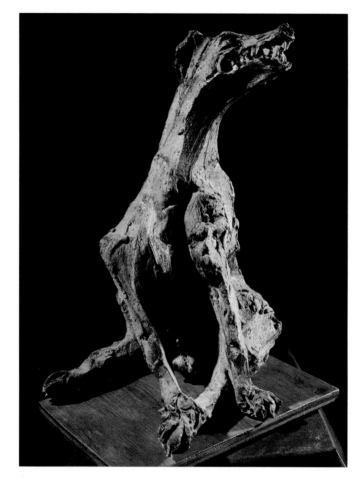

PREPARATION AND PROJECTS

Let us move on now and see what the very first steps are that you must take as you start to work. By this I do not mean what kind of workspace you should set up, where you should put your tools or how you should lay them out, nor how you should stand or sit. None of that is particularly useful information in the end because each person has his own way of doing things and his own way of living. Your work space is something only you can decide upon; there are no rules. The only truly important thing to keep in mind is that sculpture by its very nature is rather stationary. Therefore you should work someplace where you can move about easily, because you probably will not be able to move your clay, no matter what size it is. For the same reason the light should also be strong enough so that you can see all sides of your work clearly, from wherever you are standing.

As for your project, the question is slightly more complicated. It should not be difficult to understand that each time you have an idea for a project you would like to carry out, you should try to think it through with as much detail as possible. When we are talking about sculpture, the aspects and elements to consider are many. A project that is only in your head runs the risk of neglecting one aspect or another and therefore ultimately coming undone. For this reason it is always a good idea to make your first drafts on paper. This allows you to clarify just what it is you want to do and at the same time to consider all the different aspects of work involved. One or more drawings, depending on how difficult the project is, will give you the opportunity to figure out, correct and put in reciprocal relationship all of the different aspects and dimensions, the proportions of the various parts which must harmonise as a whole, perspective, the weight of the volumes and of the masses, the dynamics of the form and even what colours you will use if you decide to paint it.

Along with all of this, it would also be wise at least to consider what the ultimate destination of the object will be when it is drawn up and finished, or at least what you would like it to say.

Obviously, you will want to consider whether you intend ultimately to display the object indoors or outdoors.

In any case, this too, the "how" and "why" and "where", will come almost instinctively through your own personal tastes and awareness.

Examples of preliminary preparations and projects: the works on pages 45 and 47 were first drawn up as "sketches" in terracotta (pages 44 and 46) and then later executed by the artists in marble.

Above:
Giovan Pietro Lasagna: Design in terracotta for a relief of Sisera and Jael. *Milan, Museo del Duomo.*

Right:
Giovan Pietro Lasagna: Relief of Sisera and Jael *(1635/40). Marble. Milan, Duomo, lintel of the facade.*

46

Left:
Carlo Simonetta: Design for a relief of the
birth of St. John the Good *(1690).*
Terracotta. Milan, Museo del Duomo.

Right:
Carlo Simonetta and Stefano Sampietro:
Relief of the birth of St. John the Good
(1693). Marble. Milan, Duomo, Chapel of St.
John the Good.

47

MATERIALS AND TOOLS

Down through the ages, the artist's workshop worthy of respect has always been clean and well organised, clearly reflecting the disciplined mind of its master. This is something worth keeping in mind as you begin to model, for it is not only practical advice but good mental preparation.

Material

Natural clay is a mixture of water and earth. The kind of earth used in modelling comes from sedimentary rocks whose origins are organic. When the earth absorbs water, it becomes a plastic mass that is easy to model and keeps its shape after it dries. It is made up mainly of kaolin (aluminium silicate), silica, aluminium, iron oxide (which after firing gives terracotta its characteristic reddish colour), and other minerals like quartz and carbonates.

Its principal characteristics are its plasticity, its ability to harden, the fact that it shrinks as it dries, its porousness and its colour.

Plasticity depends mainly on how fine the granules are which make up the clay and how much water is mixed with it (the molecules of water mix with the earth to become part of the very structure of the mixture).

Hardness is obtained by firing, which eliminates the hygroscopic water, as well as by the preliminary drying process. The composition of the material itself also affects how hard it will eventually be.

Shrinkage (the contraction of the clay's mass and volume) occurs as water is eliminated and in this process, the porousness of the material is a factor. The greater the shrinkage, the less porous it is.

The addition of various additives to correct imbalances can augment or reduce one or another of the intrinsic properties of the material.

Different kinds of clay vary according to their composition, the proportions of the different substances that make them up and the presence of additives. There is enough variety in clays to satisfy the most diverse requirements and special demands of the sculptor. Because of this range, it would be useless to try to describe all the different kinds of clays available and their characteristics, given the scope of this book. It would only confuse beginners without giving them enough information to resolve their doubts. In any case, it is not necessary at this stage, when one is just starting out, to consider the question of what kind of clay to use. Ordinary clay, the kind found in any art supply or hobby shop, will be perfectly adequate for our purpose.

Tools

Four tools, similar to the ones pictured on pages 52, 53 and 54 will be more than sufficient for the beginner.

People new to a hobby or art too often want to outfit themselves with all kinds of useless and superfluous things, with the hope that thus equipped they will get better results more quickly simply because they own a vast and picturesque battery of tools. In reality, it turns out to be not only useless but also impractical to amass such sophisticated

Clay pit near Porto Torres in Sardinia, Italy.

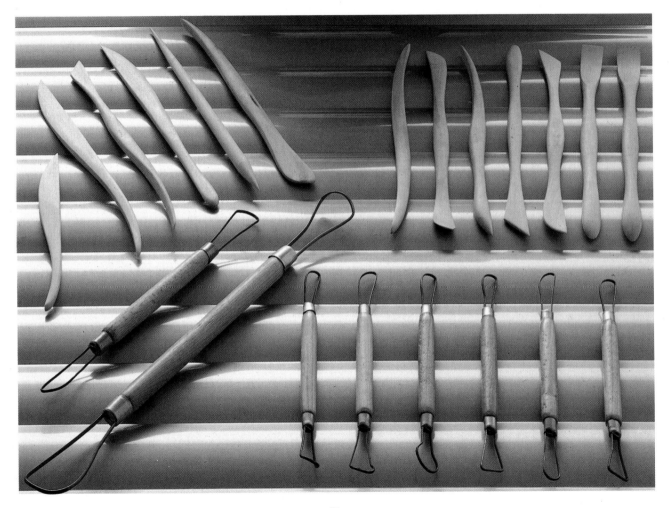

instruments. It only shows one up as a dilettante attributing powers to tools that mentally and technically one does not yet possess. This phenomenon can also be observed in young children. If you watch them when they are drawing you will notice that when they are unable to express an idea, their solution to this problem is constantly to switch crayons or pencils. For our purposes, we need only be concerned with the following:

A wire loop for modelling: two or three in different shapes and sizes should be enough;

A wooden modelling tool: you will need a pair of these wooden tools with more or less rounded tips in different sizes and shapes made of good quality wood;

A spatula or metal trowel (like the kind commonly used for plastering)

A piece of fine copper wire for cutting clay (0 less than 1 mm).

One's tools should be treated with the same respect as a public garden. Care and attention to them will result in their longevity and effectiveness.

THE HAND: A VERY SPECIAL TOOL

Now that you have your list of the four most important tools needed to begin modelling, it is time to discuss in more detail the most important tool of all, your hand.

As an instrument for shaping, the hand is the most reliable tool, ideal for a fast-working brain, which needs something equally fast to carry out its orders as they are conceived.

Modelling is essentially about adding and subtracting, although the inexperienced spend a great deal of time merely shifting the clay around with uncoordinated hands. All too often, the result is the opposite of giving form to a mass. We frequently talk about the correct positioning of the hands when, for example, we talk of a pianist---straight wrists, hands parallel and in line with the forearms.

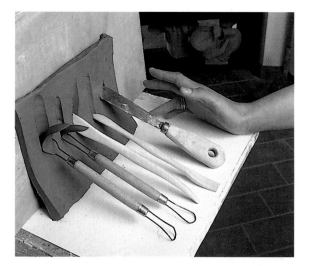

This kind of discipline is drummed in from the very beginning while the student is still practicing scales and doing simple exercises. It is a characteristic which allows one to recognise at a glance the student of a good teacher as opposed to the dilettante or one who was not properly trained. The same holds true for those who want to begin modelling. Earlier we said that it was important to start out on the right foot and begin with the right methods and discipline from the very beginning, so that the correct positioning of the hands becomes a habit, a spontaneous action reflecting one's own personal style of working. If the initial training is not thorough and solid, it becomes much harder, though not impossible, to correct bad habits further on down the road. Your work will seem harder and less fruitful and time and energy will be wasted and it will all be because you did not learn the correct procedures from the start.

Now to begin. Besides the palm of the hand, most of the time you will be using only two fingers when working with clay: the thumb and the index finger. The first important rule is to avoid "chewing" the clay with your entire hand, which you may be tempted to do initially when you still do not know what you want to do with the clay.

The functions that the thumb and index finger will be carrying out are many and therefore it is neces-

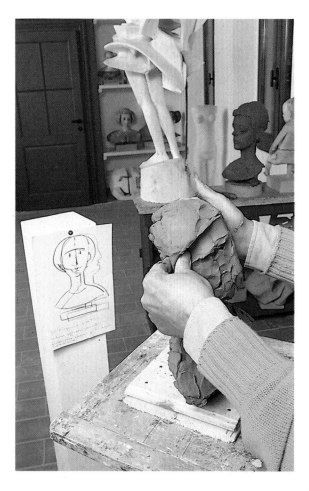

sary to learn to coordinate them. Once you know what kind of shape you want, you must think about how you want to use your fingers so that they work in a precise way, and not haphazardly. Your fingers can draw, determine planes, cut, make indentations, add, raise and above all, feel. This is what makes the hand the most precious tool that you can use. Any other tool, as adequate as it may be for what you want to do with it, will never be more than a mute passive extension or accessory to the hand.

The great tactile sensitivity which it possesses allows the hand to evaluate, weigh, measure and ascertain the state of the substance that it is touching. It is able not only to receive and interpret messages suggested from within, but it can receive and transmit a vast number in the other direction, from without. The hand is the link between the internal and the external worlds, between the objectivity of the material which it is working with and your own inner mind. It receives and furnishes data and information, it collects and delivers messages, it can even inspire. But its "intelligence" is

In the photograph, left, the correct positioning of the hands can be seen clearly. One hand works as a tool, the other supports the clay. In the photographs, right, the two hands have exchanged roles.

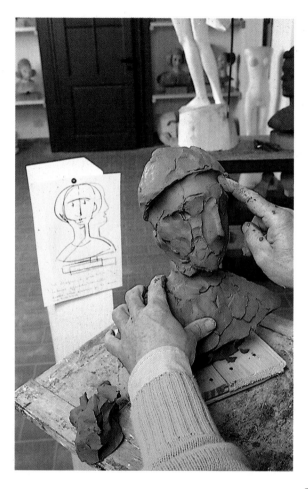

not limited to this. The hand is in fact capable of having a memory and learning from experience. Because of its tactile sensitivity it can learn to evaluate the dampness and consistency of the material and decide what to do next based on both

It is important to get into the habit of using the hands correctly from the very start. In each photo, you can see that only one hand acts as a tool, while the other keeps busy, acting as a support.

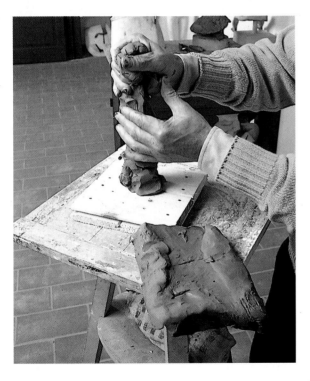

the information just obtained and the knowledge that comes with time and experience.

All these things make our hands very precious tools indeed, intelligent and ready to work.

Other tools are only necesssary when our hands, because of their shape and make-up, cannot do everything that needs to be done, such as making a fine deep incision, cleaning out a small piece of clay, or digging deep into the material. Given the proper tool, however, the hand can become long, sharp, and thin and bore deeply into the clay. Even then, the result will still be a matter of how sensitive that particular hand is, how successfully it can work and what tools it has at its disposal.

The important thing is to keep alive and direct the coordination of hand and brain, gesture and desire, action and an awareness of what must be done. It is useless to start tearing into the clay, poking one's fingers in here and there, with no apparent logic whatsoever, proceeding tentatively, in the hopes that eventually what you have in mind will miraculously emerge. Sometimes it does happen that chance produces an effect or an idea that ends up being of value (this depends on the intuition of the creator spotting and exploiting it) but it is rare and fortuitous. It cannot be relied upon if one wants to give shape to a specific idea or wish. Even the smallest action of the hand should correspond to some idea we have, it should be the result of choice, an impulse dictated by logic linked to sensitivity and experience. One should aim for and maintain a continous and tightly linked coordinated exchange between eye, mind and hand.

Nothing else is of any value if you do not keep these three points constantly in mind and related to each other. That said, I think that we can now go on and get our hands in the clay. It is time to talk about how to work with it.

The correct use of the hand as tool is clearly illustrated in the photographs on pages 58, 59, 61. Notice how in the illustration on page 59 (right) the thumb rests against the head as a kind of guide when cutting, while in the photograph on page 61 this has not been necessary.

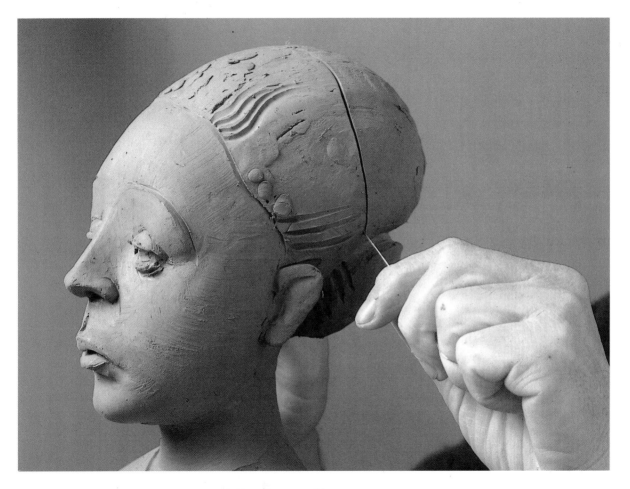

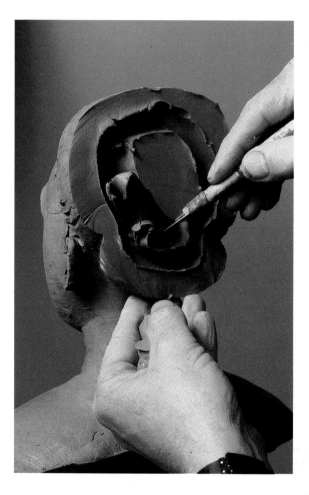

In the following photographs, the concept of the hand as tool is clearly illustrated once more. They also show how the two hands work together, one actively, the other supporting the bust.

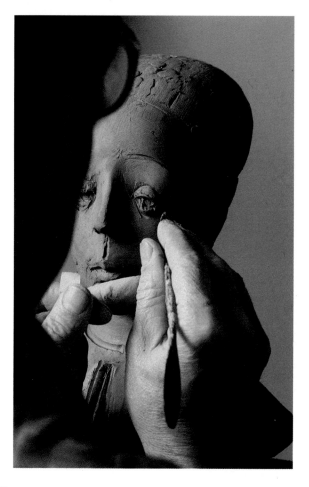

LET'S BEGIN: HOW TO MODEL CLAY

It seems almost superfluous to give etymological information on the verb "to model" for, very simply, it means "to give form".

It is an action that turns an idea, an abstract concept, into something visible and tangible, and it does this by the manipulation of a plastic material, which, in our case, is clay. In fact, according to the book of Genesis in the Bible, we ourselves are the results of some very early modelling. The act of modelling, that is, giving form to a malleable substance, would seem to be almost instinctive, an urge we have all had at one time or another. One needs only to think of children who love to play with mud or with some other soft material, or of the grandmother or cook who enjoys kneading and shaping bread into different shapes, which can be very fanciful and amusing. And of course there is another group who, having followed some instinctive impulse, bought this manual, thereby showing very clear evidence of their predisposition to modelling. To feel an interest or even a strong urge to work with clay provides the most genuine motivation for doing creative work. Heartfelt interest will provide an incentive as one learns the basic techniques.

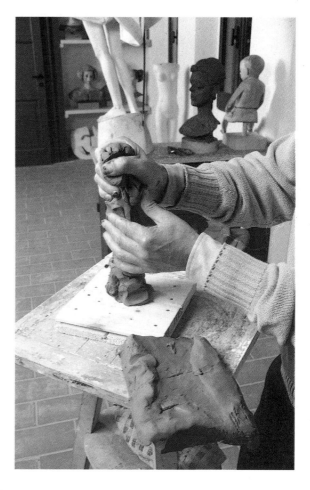

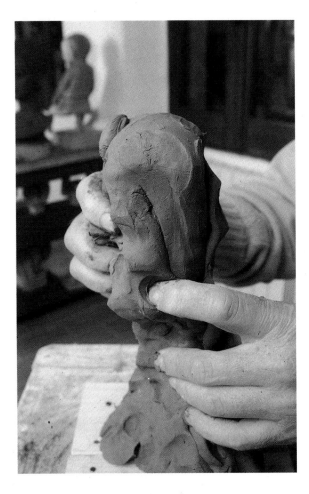

The only thing left to do before you begin to work in earnest is to learn to be a little patient, humble and disciplined in your habits so that what you do will bring you satisfying results quickly.

As you will see in the following pages, my explanation of how to work with clay is not a verbal step by step description of how to do it; there are no lessons in the strict sense of the word. Instead I have organised it to be more like a documentary. This was always my intention. So along with limited written explanations, you will find a detailed and wide-ranging sequence of photographs that are meant to show you clearly and in as graphic and all-encompassing a way as possible, everything you will need to know about the different phases of work. You will see in these pictures all the basic elements of working with clay, the ABC's of modelling, as it were. I am convinced that practical examples, that is, actually seeing what is being discussed, are the best and most direct ways of teaching these skills. As the old saying goes, one picture is worth a thousand words.

Modelling a head in the round

Now then, let us begin with our first project. I have decided to start by showing you how to model a bust, as experience has taught me that it is the subject most frequently chosen by beginners. If

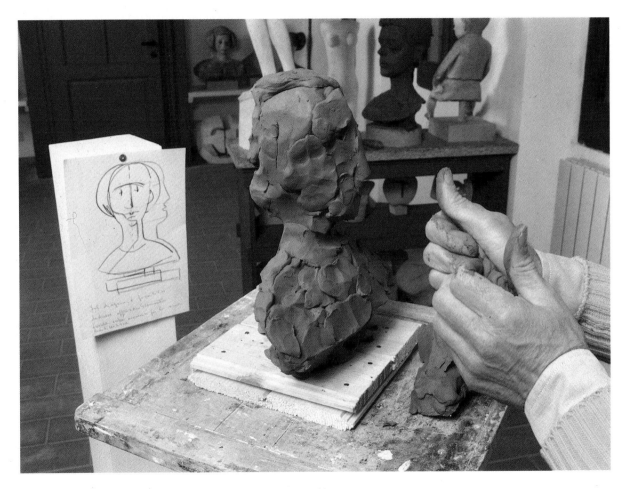

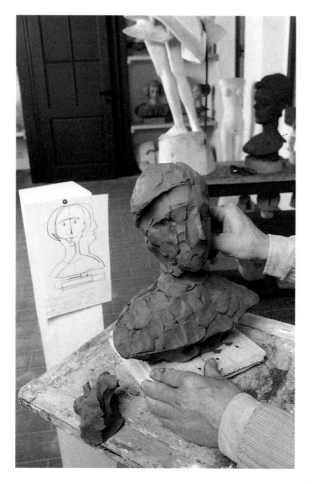

you ever have the chance to visit a kiln or firing oven, you will notice immediately if you look at all the different projects being fired, that the subject most often made by so-called dilettantes (though I like to think of them as future friends of sculpture) is the head. One has to wonder why. I think it happens because our budding sculptors believe, perhaps a bit naively, that they will get the quickest and most successful results by modelling something that they think they know best and are most familiar with, namely the face.

Reality is a little bit different. There is nothing in fact more fascinating but at the same time more complicated and exacting than a face, ever changing and ever different, revealing an inexhaustible range of expressions and attitudes as fleeting as a glance and over in an instant. Once one is aware of this it is not difficult to understand how complicated a portrait can become when the subject one intends to reproduce is not just a face from our fantasy but meant to be the portrait of an actual person.

Here I would like to make a short and simple deviation on the subject.

Paradoxically, a portrait is in fact a kind of theft. It is an attempt, one not always destined to be successful, to capture the moment, a state of mind, that the subject of the sculpture has betrayed for an instant and allows to be caught. These brief

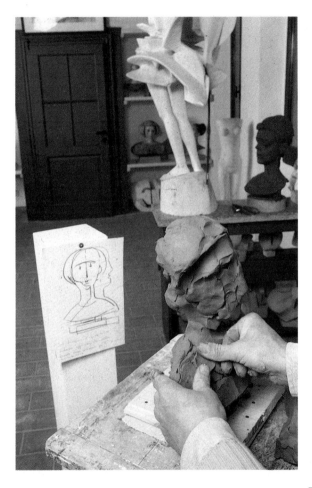

moments, these wordless communications revealed from time to time, are glimpses into the character of a person, revelations of his state of mind. In an attempt truly to portray character, and not just a face, your goal should be to try to capture something more than just a mere physical resemblance. If you only concentrate on a physical likeness, you may end up with a certain similarity, it may even be relatively satisfactory, but you will never capture the spirit, the soul of your subject. Clearly, if all you want is to get a close likeness of your subject's features, you will do just as well with a plaster cast (pop-art has provided us with endless examples of this approach). But an operation like that will never be able to give you that mysterious and indefinable something which is the essence of real human expression. This can only be achieved, even when done with artifice and imitation, by those who learn how to look and to see, to go beyond the limits of apparent reality. Today now that the very function of the portrait has changed so completely, this is truer than ever.

At one time portraying a person was a way of documenting and preserving his or her image, a way of fixing it in time and keeping it alive. The

In yet another project, we can again see how the two hands work together as tool and support.

71

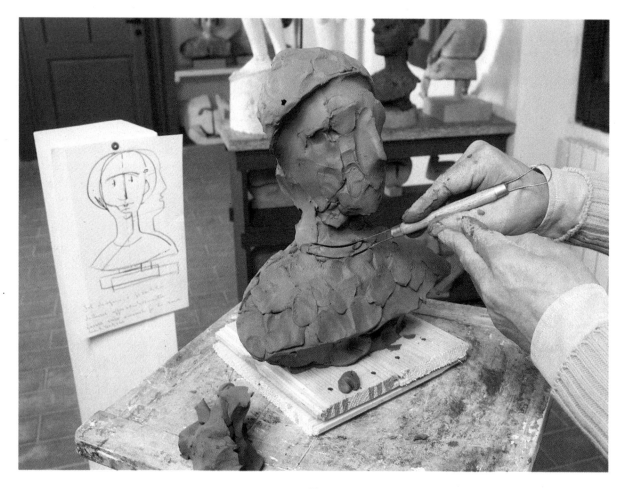

If you must interrupt your work, make sure that you cover it so that the surface does not dry out and you can continue working on it later. To do this, cover it completely with a damp cloth, draping it over the surface (left). Then cover the cloth with a piece of plastic, (a trash bag works well), and tie a string around the base so that it stays tightly wrapped keeping the cloth inside damp (right).

portrait was an historical yet familiar kind of document, proof that a person had existed and that they looked a certain way, in a certain place and that they had certain belongings, which were often also faithfully reproduced. It was meant to be a measure of their social position and prestige.

Those who by social position and by tradition owned portraits and had portraits made of themselves, were also those who were able to live on in the memory of the world.

The world today has gone through profound changes in its social customs and structures, especially in the world of technology. What was once achieved and preserved with a portrait is today the work of a photograph. It is the photograph now which provides us with the means to remember, document and preserve our past. But photography is limited. It can only reproduce an image, it cannot interpret. The way I see it, once we accept the challenge of doing a portrait, our search for the essence of our subject will be very similar to any psychological study. The only difference will be that the result will be in clay instead of on paper.

All this is true of course only if you want to make the effort to carry out what has traditionally been defined as sculpture.

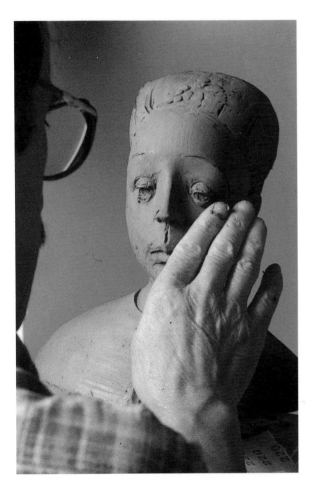
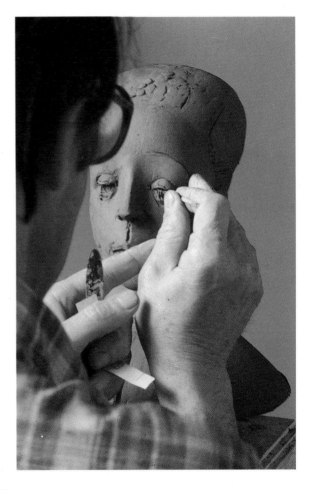

77

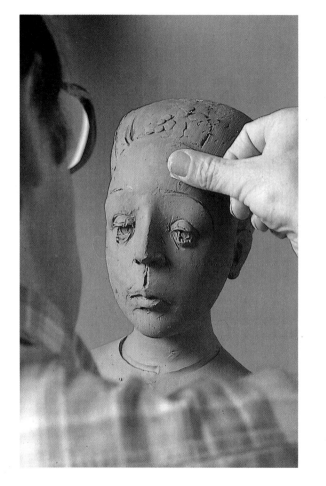

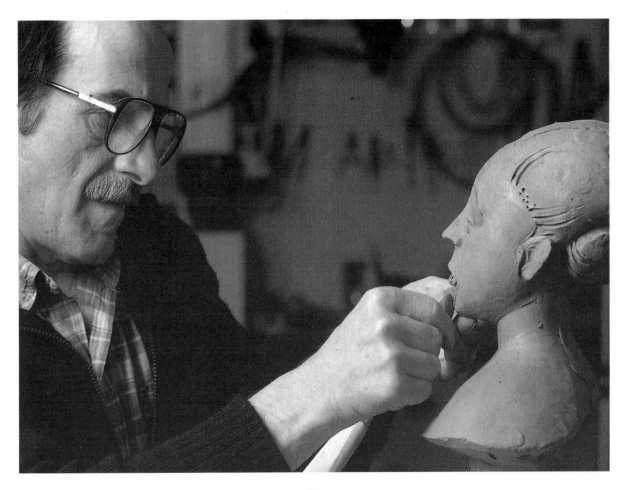

Left, you can see the fully modelled head, ready for firing, which is the next stage.

80

Relief

A sculpture made in relief at first glance would seem to be simpler than making something fully in the round. However, this can be misleading. While some of the practical aspects may be simpler, it is certainly not true of the conceptual side of it. That said, if you look at the photographs in this book you will see that the basic steps are fairly simple. Any surface can act as a support to hold a layer of clay on which to outline your composition and develop the images that you want to portray. Once you find a smooth flat surface for the clay, you can begin to draw (draw, always draw) your subject right away. Then you simply add clay until you reach the level of relief you want.

Relief gives the illusion that it is very easy to do, because it seems more like a molded drawing than a real sculpture. This is not true. It is actually a greatly reduced version of sculpture in the round with all the same values. In short, it is the synthesis of them within the restricted space and reduced thickness that they encompass. With relief, volume as a value often plays a reduced role and therefore, the contrast between planes can end up almost non-existent. What differences there are, however, should be maintained, even when they are very slight or reduced to a minimum. One should avoid working against this by cutting into the surface of a

work, and turn instead to other solutions to maintain relief such as the use of perspective. Perspective, as we all know, is part of the art of drawing and in fact composing and expressing oneself through the technique of relief (because it is indeed a technique) demands some sort of drawing skills. Relief can be seen as a synthesis of two arts, because it combines the illusory nature of drawing and the tangible concreteness of sculpture. It is born of the symbiosis of volume with its three-dimensional modelling, and perspective, which is a rationalised representation of something, an optical illusion. Because drawing plays such an important role in the art of relief, it is very important to keep in mind what I urged above, namely, to draw, draw, draw.

If you are interested in seeing the work of someone who was and remains the best example of this art, look to Donatello....And do not forget Pisanello, with his marvellous medallions.

The photographs here and on the preceding pages document the successive phases of a panel in relief. The process starts with a sketch on paper which is then drawn onto the clay and modelled and finally the whole piece is fired.

FIRING

Once you have finished modelling your clay and given it its final shape, you must prepare it for firing. This phase is necessary if you want to keep and protect it so that its shape and surface remain intact. Firing makes the modelling material much more resistant and lightweight and brings out its characteristic colour wherein grey becomes red. However, one cannot always simply wait for the clay to dry completely and then fire it. Although small sculptures (h. 10/15 or h. 25/30 cm) can be fired as solid pieces of clay, larger sculptures need to be hollowed out before they can undergo this process. So next we will look at this operation and why it is necessary to do it.

When we speak of hollowing out a sculpture we are talking about removing clay from the inside of the piece until a shell of uniform thickness is left, approximately one or two centimeters thick.

We do this to prevent the sculpture from exploding during firing. This kind of accident can happen quite easily during firing and it mostly occurs when there are damp bits of clay remaining inside the object or when impurities in the clay such as fragments of chalk, pieces of wood and metal or some other material have been overlooked and allowed to remain in the clay. This is one reason that I urge you to be very clean, organised, and disciplined in your work, because it helps to avoid or at least to limit the risks of accidents that could easily destroy something on which you have spent a long time working.

Hollowing out an object can be a delicate operation but with practice, it should not pose any serious problems.

The first thing to do is to make a cut, using the copper wire in such as way as to remove a section of the head by opening up a kind of window or hole. Naturally you will want to make this incision in an inobtrusive place so that you do not harm the appearance of your work. For instance, you would not want to cut through any of the important or delicate areas, such as the face in a bust. When you make the cut, do it confidently and quickly so that you do not create jagged edges or damage the two sides. This is important because later, when the piece has been hollowed out, the cap you have removed must be replaced.

After you have removed a section of the head, make an outline in the cap a little way from the edge (see the photographs on pages 88 and 89)

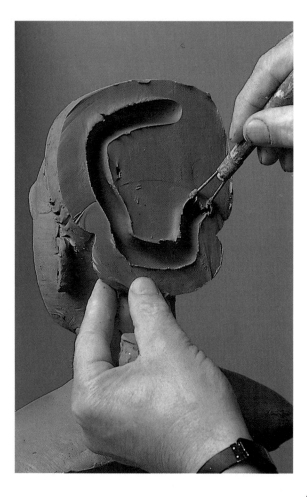
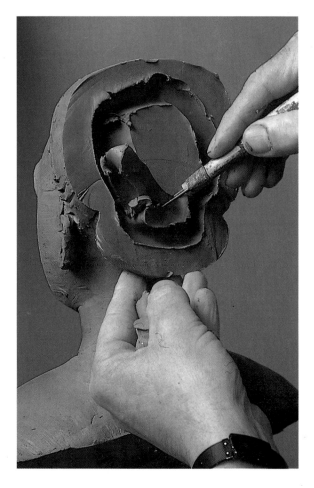

and begin to remove the clay within that outline, digging it out gently and carefully.

Once you have carved out the clay from the cap, you can go ahead and dig out the clay inside the main part of your sculpture. You will eventually come to the inner support (in the case of the bust in the photographs, it is the neck). Work carefully around it and when you have removed enough clay from the main part, insert a small piece of clay between the inner surface of the by now mostly hollowed out part of the sculpture and the upper part of the support. Then with the hollow section of the sculpture and the support once again connected you can remove the last bits of clay still sticking to the inner support in the lower half of the main section. When all the superfluous clay has been removed, it is time to reconnect the two hollowed out parts, the cap and the main section. You should have ready a bowl of water mixed with a little clay. Use enough clay so that the mixture is rather mushy and batter-like. This mixture will act as an adhesive or glue. With the help of a brush, you can use it to put the two pieces of the sculpture that you had cut apart earlier back together again. If you have cut them correctly, they should fit together perfectly, like pieces of a puzzle. When the two pieces are back in place, clean them, touching up the line where they were cut and

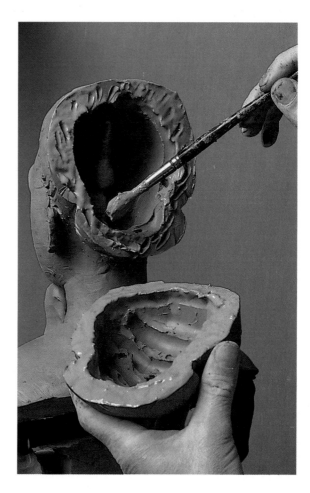

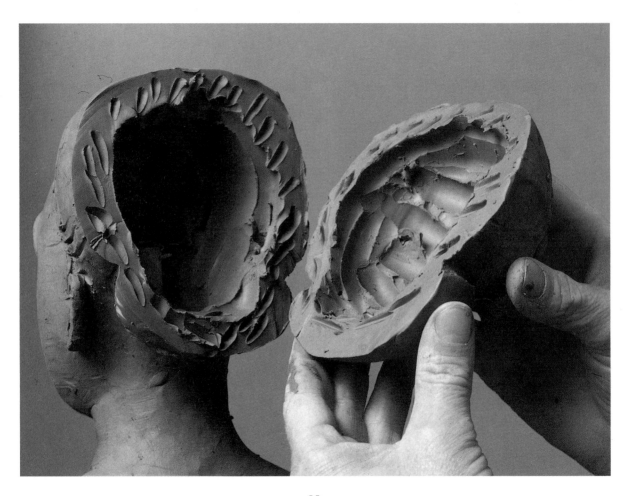

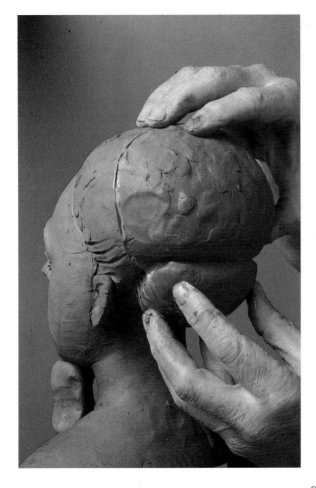

91

smoothing out any uneven edges. After you have finished all these different steps, it is time to let your sculpture dry.

Leave your sculpture somewhere where it is sheltered from strong currents of air. Such currents would speed up the process of drying too quickly and cause the clay to dry unevenly. It is even more important to keep the clay away from any source of direct heat. Leave your work untouched for at least ten days or more, depending on how big the piece is and always take into account what the surrounding atmosphere is like. As for the actual firing, conventional wisdom suggests that in most cases it is safer to rely upon those who have the proper equipment and experience with the process for they are most likely to provide the best results. This usually means taking your work to be fired at a reliable kiln. As you become more experienced and acquire more skills, it is not impossible that you will someday want to carry out this last phase yourself, but for the moment, you must be content with making the cake and taking it to the baker's for baking, as it were, just as our grandmothers used to do with their cooking.

Firing a work yourself is not a very good idea for a whole series of reasons. The best reason is that it costs a great deal of money to buy the right kind of equipment, and the right equipment requires a

good deal of space to put it in as well. In an effort to economise, equipping yourself on a shoestring is also counterproductive and very binding. An oven that is too small would always limit you to working on very small items. Another consideration to keep in mind is that for this kind of operation or, for that matter, anything to do with art, there are no precise scientific instruments or exact rules to follow that can tell you exactly what to do to get the effect you want. If you visit a kiln you will quickly become aware of just how many things there are to know about in order to fire clay: how to use the kiln, for example, what temperatures to use, the positioning of the objects inside the oven, the way to handle terracotta so as not to damage it and many other factors that must be taken into account. With no fixed rules and no machines to measure different phases and processes, as I have already said, all knowledge and skill comes from long professional experience. It is through experience that the operator knows how to solve a wide range problems as they come up. For all of these reasons, it is highly advisable when you are firing your object that you turn to those with long experience in doing it. If it is any consolation to you, it is something that even professional sculptors do, and it is also the safest way to preserve the effort and inspiration you have put into the work.

AND FINALLY, COLOUR

I have always found the subject of colour a particularly interesting one and certainly one that deserves at least a few words. So let us consider it for a moment.

What do we mean by colour?

Colour is the means by which we can reproduce the chromatic sensations that our eyes distinguish. Because the range of colours that surrounds us is extremely vast and complex, in order to figure out the best way to reproduce them, we must first understand something about the products that are available for that purpose. We will be mainly interested in two types of colours, pigments and dyes.

Pigments

Pigments are coloured substances which are transformed into insoluble powders. When mixed with a binder they can be fixed onto a support (cloth, paper, cardboard, wood, etc.).

The colours used in oils, tempera, watercolours and acrylics may all have the same origins, but they end up in very different forms because of the binders used in making each of them.

Pigments can be extracted from the mineral world, the vegetable world or the animal world. These days they are also made synthetically as well. Among the inorganic natural pigments are the natural earths and ochre, which produce yellow ochre, raw and burnt sienna, raw and burnt umber and terre verte. Inorganic synthetic pigments are extracted using the chemical processes of precipitation, sublimation and the chemical breakdown of metals.*

*Whites

Zinc white *is a pigment that gives the most brilliant white in existence, but also the least coverage. Discovered at the beginning of the 19th century, it is non-toxic. It is a white with a slightly bluish cast which mixes well with other colours, lightening them and giving them more brilliance.*

Titanium white *is a dioxide of titanium. It is a pigment invented at the beginning of this century that has gradually begun to replace all the other whites because of its superior covering ability and its purity.*

Barite white *is a barium sulphate which is also non-toxic. When mixed with zinc sulphide, barite white produces a colourant which can be used with watercolours in cases where zinc white would not be suitable or possible.*

*Yellows

Cadmium yellow *is a cadmium sulphide. Cadmium yellow is preferred to other yellows because it has no particular drawbacks. Its tonality ranges from lemon yellow to orange.*

Yellow ochre *and* Mars yellow, *extracted from ferric oxides, are more or less yellow depending on the amount of iron they contain.*

*Greens

Emerald green *is an extract of a hydrated chromium oxide obtained through calcification. It is a transparent colour with little colouring power.*

Chromium oxide green, *unlike emerald green, covers very well, but its tone is not as bright.*

Cobalt green *is a mixture of cobalt and zinc oxides and comes in various tones of green.*

*Reds

Cadmium red *is a sulphoselenide of cadmium that mixes well with cadmium yellow and is very brilliant. The amount of selenium it contains determines its shade, which can range from orange to purple.*

Cimabar red *or* Vermilion, *a mercuric sulphide, is a very old red, perhaps the oldest of all. A natural red, it now often replaces cadmium red. Most of the cimabar red mines which were around Cyprus, are now nearly depilated.*

*Blues

Cobalt blue, *a cobaltous aluminate, is obtained by the calcination of cobalt salts with aluminium. Cobalt blue is a very brilliant pigment but with only poor to average covering power.*

Prussian blue, *a ferric ferrocyanide, is not always easy available. When mixed with cadmium yellow, it produces very beautiful greens. Discovered around 1750, it has very good covering qualities.*

Ultramarine blue *is a a polysulphide of sodium alumino-silicate. It replaces the old natural ultramarine blue which was made by crushing lapis lazuli into a fine powder.*

*Violets

Cobalt violet, *a cobalt phosphate, has very little covering ability but it is very resistant to light.*

*Browns

The browns *range from raw sienna to burnt sienna, raw umber to burnt umber, and so on.*

*Blacks

Ivory black, *extracted from the oxidation of ivory, is an elusive colour today. It has been replaced by bone black which comes from the oxidation of animal bones. It is a lovely warm black but one that dries slowly.*

Vine black is made from the calcination of vine branches which are then pulverised and dried until a black powder with a bluish tint is obtained.

*Organic pigments

The organic pigments come in an enormous range of tones with great brilliance and very good covering ability compared to the inorganic pigments, which possess a relatively weak colouring ability with less brilliant tones.

Like the inorganic pigments, the organic pigments cover the whole spectrum of colours. Unlike the inorganic pigments, however, they are made from petroleum-based chemicals and make up a modest number of chemical classifications:

The aniline dyes ("azos") which range from yellows to reds and clarets.

The anthracene pigments which cover a wide range from yellows to reds and blues.

The copper phthalocyanine pigments which run from blue to green. They are very light resistant and often replace inorganic colours because of their brilliance.

The quinacridone pigments which run from pink to red to violet and include a range of colours that do not exist among the inorganic colours.

The dioxazine pigments are very light-resistant and include a range of violets that go beyond the quinacridone pigments.

*Tempera colours

A generic name, tempera refers to all the techniques which use something other than a drying oil as a binder. In the past, tempera was made with eggs, waxes or glues. Of the three, egg tempera was the most refined. Wax tempera was made by melting wax in a bain-marie along with glycerine and a few drops of ammonia. This very delicate tempera was common during the Middle Ages.

Tempera made with glue, called gouache, was the result of mixing pigments with fish or rabbit glue and then thinning the result with water. Gouache at one time was not considered a very refined tempera. Its characteristic quality was that it was quick-drying and thus could be used for sketches or rough drafts. Today it has become the only tempera sold.

Dyes

These are soluble coloured substances which can penetrate or be absorbed by a support. Vegetable and animal dyes were known in Egypt four thousand years ago. Towards the second half of the 19th century aniline dyes were invented and since then they have been widely used. In the world of art, dyes can be produced that have the same range of tones as pigments. They are sold in the form of dry cakes or come in tubes as a kind of thick paste and must then be diluted with water, alchohol, etc.

22 MaiMeRi
18 MaiMeRi 982
12 MaiMeRi 982
10 MaiMeRi 982 SETOLA
6 MaiMeRi 982 SETOLA
4 MaiMeRi 982 SETOLA
2 MaiMeRi 982 SETOLA

Many people believe that colour has no place in sculpture. They see it as simply an indulgence, an extra something added on and they therefore dismiss it as mere adornment, decorating the surface in a very superficial way, with no particular merit in and of itself. It is true that when one thinks of sculpture, the image one normally has is of a monochromatic object, at its best in black or white marble, red terracotta, or gleaming bronze. But this is simple prejudice, a subjective view which is the result of an age-old tradition, encouraged by art historians, who value form and volume above all in this branch of art and for the most part ignore colour except as it is related to the raw material of the sculpture.

If you think back, however, to classic sculpture, especially to the ancient Greeks, you will realise that this is a mistaken idea for their sculptures were often highly coloured. Unfortunately over the centuries their surfaces have been robbed of their colours, so that we can no longer see them as they were originally. However, we do know that they were conceived and made to be painted, and colour was as essential a part of their design as form, giving them a liveliness which fit in well with the world for which they were made.

Unfortunately, later generations contemplating antiquity, and especially the classical period, have chosen to ignore the fact that these sculptures were meant to be coloured and instead interpreted this lack of colour not as a loss or a consequence of the passage of time, but as the way classical sculpture was meant to be.

This is why the various periods of classicism in the Renaissance and the seventeenth century, and of neoclassicism at the end of the eighteenth century, which was a reworking of the classical tradition or, more generally, ancient art, produced sculpture that was almost exclusively deprived of colour.

If we think of the works of the master sculptors, artists like Michelangelo, Bernini and Canova, who represented, even defined the character of the art of their era, we think of sculpture completely devoid of colour. In reality, artists and sculptors considered the use of colour completely natural and used it as one more aspect of their work, and not only in remote times. During the Middle Ages and up until the beginning of the fifteenth century, wooden sculpture as well as majolica and glazed terracotta (Luca della Robbia) were always painted with colours. However, large statues, which were the most highly valued and best-known sculptures, were made without colour. In fact, the image that comes to mind most often when we think of sculpture is of something that is basically white. For this reason, sculpture today is expected to be white with only a few variations, depending on the material used. At least this is true for most people. And yet, as we have seen, this idea of white or at least monochromatic sculpture is essentially the result of prejudice, however justifiable, by those who preceded us and passed on to us their interpretation, a reading which if not wrong, at least was distorted and absolute, to the point that for centuries, and even today, it bound and restricted our very concept of sculpture as an art that did not require any use of colour.

In reality, colour should be an integral part of sculpture for it works to underline its plasticity, circumscribing the volumes and playing up the most expressive parts of the subject. Think of the mouth, the eyes and all the details of the complexion to which the author has attributed a special narrative interest.

Not least in importance is the problem of placement, that is, the need to make the subject "come alive" in its own environment, putting it in dialectic rapport with space, with the world it was intended for. Because colour is obvious and direct, a characteristic that can be understood easily, it allows the subject to explain itself naturally, within its context, yet without overwelming. Particular attention should therefore be given to the use of

colour; it should not just be seen as a finishing touch or a minor operation left to the very end.

However, the use of colour is a very personal choice and it is undoubtedly optional, dependent, of course, on the nature of the project and the sensitivity of the artist. Nevertheless, when one must decide whether one wishes to add this dimension to a project, one should not just decide haphazardly.

At this point you would do well to work bearing a couple of very general ideas in mind. These ideas should in no way restrict your freedom of expression nor impinge on your personal tastes, but on the contrary, help to encourage them.

The application and above all the choice of one colour rather than another should never overwelm or work against the nature of the project being worked on. To put this another way, a work with a strong character and accentuated plasticity will not need to have these values excessively underlined by adding colour, since they will already be stressed by the sculpture itself.

On the other hand, colour can be helpful in the case of a sculpture with minimum relief. It will not add much to the sense of relief since the artist very probably intended it to be the way it was, but it can be used to illuminate the surface of the work, for example, or to accentuate the lines of construction

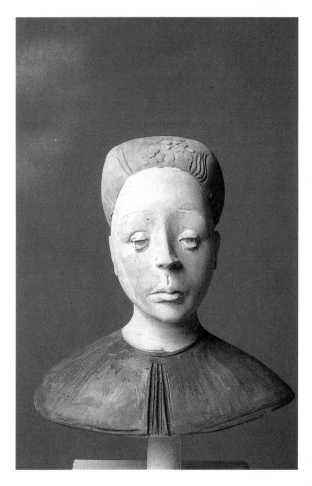

and to highlight and indicate special details.

Colour should never look as if it were added as an afterthought or applied simply to cover and hide the sculpture, as an extraneous addition. Instead it should be an integral and decisive part of the whole concept, one more form of communication. This means trying to make it seem as if it is part of the essence of the subject, not an additional factor brought in that remains on the surface. Colour should be seen as a kind of light, a part of the material itself, not simply covering its surface but seeming to originate from within. Ultimately, in fact, that is what it must be, the light of the material, born from within (or seeming to be) and acting as an integral part of the sculpture, rather than a component applied externally as a simple decorative addition.

In this way, colour plays its own precise narrative role. It cannot exist on its own but it is nevertheless part of the whole statement, on a par with the other formal and expressive elements of the sculpture as an important characteristic.

This said, I hope I have convinced you of both the richness and the weight of the contribution that colour offers, what possibilities and implications it holds, the tasks that it can carry out, and the functions which from time to time or in a particular situation it can accomplish.

As for the ways in which colour can be used, it can give an emotional character and flavour to a work, or it can act as a naturalistic component. In quite the opposite way, colour can be used to distance the subject from reality, making it something purely fanciful and imaginative. Beside these possibilities, colour can also provide a means by which one can accentuate the formal or plastic values of a work while at the same time making what it is trying to communicate both personal and original. For this reason, it is very important that as much care and attention is given to this aspect of the sculpture as to all the other phases of work, i.e., the drawing, the composition, the construction and the modelling.

Another important aspect is what, for want of another word, I would call the "correct measure," that is, determining occasionally how incidental the use of colour should be.

The ideal, of course, would be to proceed with caution, even to be somewhat miserly, adding only a little colour at a time so that you can establish just when enough has been applied, that is, the exact point at which the right intensity has been reached, as well as the desired density. For this reason you should always apply colour in thin washes over paint that is already dry. By applying it carefully in successive layers of diluted colour you

can gradually build up to the desired tone.

It is useful, I think, to remember that a sculpture is something that is alive and breathes and as such it should be respected. The subject that we are working on has its own skin with all the vibrant sensitivity of the model. It is a "skin" which we should take care not to suffocate by covering it with a thick layer of paint, thereby masking it and destroying everything that is fresh and vital about it. Colour should emerge as a part of the basic material, as if it were a natural part of it with its own relevant character.

Having made all this clear, let us see just how to carry out this last phase of work, in an orderly fashion.

At this stage you should have your piece of terracotta fired. A lovely warm red, its surface will be porous almost to the point of dustiness. If you try to apply paint to it directly, you run the risk of the terracotta absorbing the paint very quickly, so that it spots and you are unable to get a smooth homogeneous layer. It is a bit like using watercolour paints directly on a dry piece of paper. The first brush strokes are quickly absorbed, instantly permeating a very absorbent surface, and later there is no way to draw the colour back out so that it ends up creating an intensely coloured blot. How can you avoid this? In fact it is very simple. You must

create a suitable base to receive the coloured solution, so that it becomes a genuine support.

There is a very easy way to make the surface impermeable to successive layers of paint. All you have to do is cover the surface with a soft brush dipped into whole milk (milk contains casein, the property of which is impermeability). Then repeat this operation two or three more times at least; this will be sufficient to prevent the virgin terracotta from absorbing colour too quickly and you will avoid the inconvenience of not being able to continue on a uniformly thick and even surface. Of course you must be careful to apply the milk evenly, covering every surface including the inevitable cracks and joints, so that you do not leave some areas uncovered that will then be more absorbent than others.

Now let us turn to the kinds of colours which can be used for painting. Ordinary ready-made tempera is one of the best, as are pigments made from natural coloured powders.

Tempera does not need anything added to it as it is already prepared with a fixative. However, if you are using pigments, the addition of a fixative is necessary. A good one to use is one like Elmer's Glue or white glue diluted in water at a ratio of 1:10 or even better a very dilute solution of shellac and denatured alcohol. The latter needs a few days

to dissolve completely and blend, but it can be prepared in large batches and stored for use again at some later date as long as it is kept in a tightly closed container. Otherwise, as alcohol is very volatile, there is always the risk that when you go to use it, you will find there is none left. Once the colors are ready, as mentioned, you can then move on to applying them. Of course, each layer of colour must be completely dry before the next one is applied in order not to turn the surface into paste. You should also be careful that you do not go back over brushstrokes freshly laid down; otherwise you will create a build-up of colour in one place.

Once the desired tones have been achieved and all the small touches added, it is necessary to wait for at least two hours for the paint to dry. Then you can take a natural sponge dipped in a solution of alcohol and shellac or water and white glue and very gently go over the painted surface with this solution. When you have done this you should leave your work for a few days so the paint can dry completely.

When it is thoroughly dry, sprinkle the surface of the terracotta with alcohol and then with a match light the alcohol. Naturally you must be very careful when you do this. (Just in case, it would be wise to keep the telephone number of the fire

department close by...) The alcohol will burn with a low blue flame until all of it is consumed. Once the flames go out, the colour is set. Now all that is left is the last stage of finishing or polishing.

For this you must get hold of some ordinary yellow floor wax or one of the more fluid furniture waxes containing beeswax, the more of it, the better. Once again using a soft brush, apply a generous layer over the entire painted surface. Then with a good woolen cloth (an old scarf would be ideal), rub the surface until you obtain the shine you want.

And that's it. At this stage I hope that my suggestions, the accompanying photographs, and your own experience will lead you to enjoyment and satisfaction as you model clay. Good luck.

MORE USEFUL EXAMPLES

So far, I have given you two very detailed examples of working with clay, one explaining how to model a head in the round and one describing how a small piece in relief is made. But, of course, there are practically endless possibilities with sculpture. Certainly fantasy and inventiveness are very important, but they are something you must develop yourself. What I would like to show you next briefly is how to work with figures in different poses that might inspire you with ideas for projects of your own.

The illustrations that follow have been drawn in the style of a collage, using different colours, so that you can see clearly and schematically how to work, not just with a head, but with a whole figure. By looking carefully at the drawings, you should be able to see how to construct and arrange the figure in various poses.

Look first at the examples and then try to work out in your own mind how they have been put together. You will quickly see that there is a certain logic to them, which, once you have figured it out, will stand you in good stead, for it can be applied to all sorts of forms and figures, not just the ones in the pictures.

What exactly can be learned by careful study of the illustrations that follow? Let us take a look at them.

The first important lesson you can learn is how to use supports. There are many kinds of supports, but in each case, they consist of two essential parts, a base (usually a flat piece of wood) and another piece to keep the figure upright. The latter can also be made of wood, which is what was used with the head modelled earlier in the book, or it can be a piece of metal or even clay. The appearance may change, but its purpose always remains the same: to give support to the sculpture as a whole. For this reason, it is placed so that it props up the main axes, that is, the main lines of construction holding the object together. Let us look now in more detail.

In illustration number 4 (page 115) you will see a standing figure. The lines of this figure are essentially vertical and the support is placed above the two legs. Here you run into the problem of having the more fragile limbs being forced to carry the weight of the trunk, which is more compact and heavier than they are.

The black lines show the shape and path of the

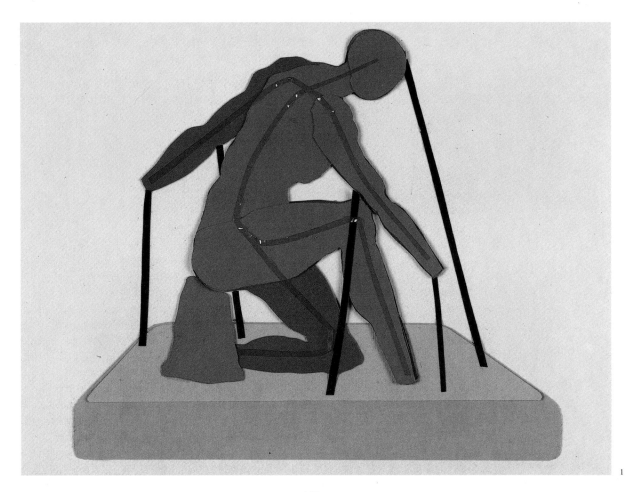

support, preferably a metal one, as it goes into the body of the figure and then turns upwards towards the head. This solution makes it possible to support and hold erect an elongated and delicate figure vertically with minimal support at the base. As for the legs, they do not rest directly on the base but on an additional clay form. This serves as a solid anchor until the work is finished, at which point it will be cut away from the limbs with a copper wire, separating the legs from their support. As the clay dries, it shrinks somewhat, as you will have seen when you worked with the head, and as a result you will find that the legs pull away slightly from the base. If you want to make this kind of support, you will need an iron rod about 4 to 6 mm in diameter, depending of course on the dimensions of the sculpture and its weight. It is very important that the rod be rounded, with a smooth surface. A few days after you have finished

1. For this kind of pose, a support made of clay and placed at the base of the trunk should be sufficient; there it will carry the greatest load. For the arms, the four supports, indicated in black, are placed at the elbows and the wrists. For this particular pose I have also added one to hold up the head, as, left unsupported, its weight might pull it down and fracture or crack the base of the neck.

your modelling, but before the clay has begun to shrink, while it is still of a manageable consistency and can be supported without damaging its shape or the surface, you should insert the rod, rotating it as you move it towards the top of the figure. Then the figure can be laid down carefully on a flat surface to finish drying. A smooth rounded rod is important because if the support is not smooth and cylindrical, it will not be possible to insert it into your sculpture without using force and very possibly breaking it.

In figures 1 and 3 (pages 110 and 114) you can see that one of the supports has been made with a bit of clay which can, at the last moment, be cut away. As it turns out, the poses of these two figures make them much more compact, and the points of contact with the base cover a much larger surface area. In figure 3, the bulk of the weight comes from the pelvis; below it has been placed a clay support. There are no particular problems with supports or reinforments in the second example either, because the figure is lying down and rests almost completely along the horizontal plane of the base. As you can see, it is easy to establish what kind of support to use if you keep in mind the demands you will be making on it. Again I would like to remind you of the importance of thinking through your project and as part of that, making use of a preliminary drawing to figure out the particular needs and structural demands of your subject as well as establishing the kinds of supports it will need and their placement.

There are other things that can be observed in these examples too. We have seen how to sustain the sculpture with supports which will then preserve the shape of the sculpture until it is finished. But we can see in the other examples that there are often other parts that stick out and hang suspended in the air, and in doing so they end up extended some way from the central axis. If you leave them as they are, without any prop to hold them up you run the risk of having them fall off or droop, especially when the clay is still wet. Thus, you will need something to shore them up as well. In the illustrations you will see that I have indicated these supports either as black rods or as small bits of clay placed under the figure. Their function is that of holding up all the various projecting parts. Whether they are pencils or small wooden rods is not important but it is important that their bases always rest on small pieces of clay. The clay of the sculpture will shrink as it dries and so will the clay below the support. The wood of course will not, so if the wooden supports do not have any clay placed under them, they may end up falling out as the clay above them contracts or they

may be difficult to remove later without damaging the sculpture itself. It is very important to remember this when you are working with your supports. For the parts closest to the base (for example, the left foot in figure 3) a piece of clay is sufficient. In fact, it should be easy to figure out where the supports should go by looking at the examples.

The last thing that the illustrations show is a reddish line that runs the length of the body, through the arms and legs, uninterrupted. It exemplifies a concept, valid for every project, for any kind of application, that is perhaps harder to explain than to understand. But I will try briefly to make it clear. The reddish line indicates the continuity of the movement of the clay, a cohesive force that

2. This pose does not present any particular problems with support. The reclining figure rests for the most part along the horizontal plane of the base. Four rods to hold up the extended arm and the leg should be enough (one at the wrist, one at the elbow, one at the knee and one at the ankle). The two parts of the left arm and leg that are slightly raised have been supported with small balls of clay. Particular care should be taken with the more fragile parts, in this case, the extended arm and leg, and the head, which is given extra support with a rod. In this figure, it is the back of the head that needs support, not the front as in the previous one.

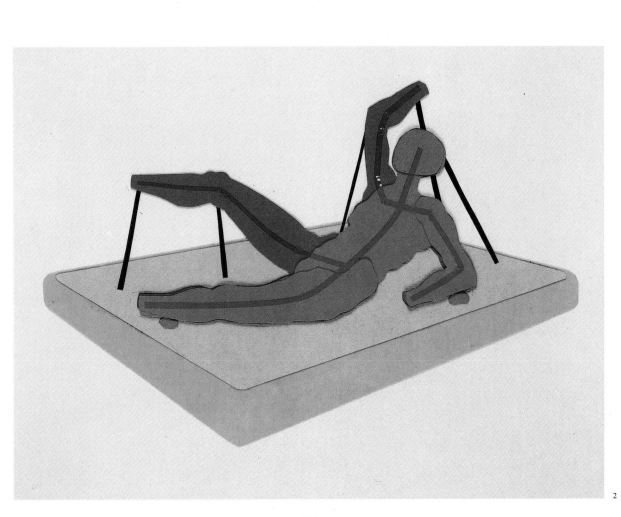

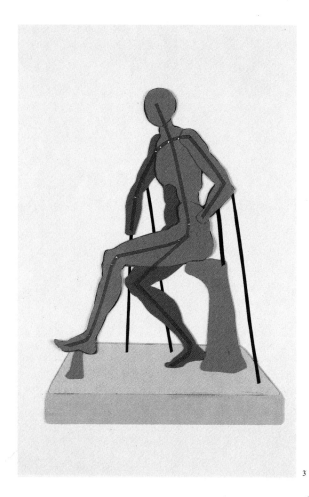

must not be interrupted. What does this mean? It is simple. It means that one should never build a model in segments that are then stuck together, but rather that the basic structure, the initial construction should be one single uninterrupted piece. By this I mean that when you are modelling the legs or the arms you should not stick them on as separate pieces. Instead they should be part of a long strip of clay, a sort of rod that will be the basic structure for the limbs, an uninterrupted line that you can then model, adding the details and whatever else you like.

If you build the figure in segments, even though it might seem easier, it will ultimately weaken the clay by creating separate zones which may end up being fractured because you will have compromised the continuity and the strength of the

3. In this illustration, you see a seated figure. This pose does not present any particular problems of support either. A large piece of clay is used as a support for the trunk, four rods hold up the arms, placed as you can see in the illustration. Attention must only be paid to the anchoring of the raised left foot. A piece of clay holds it in place.

3

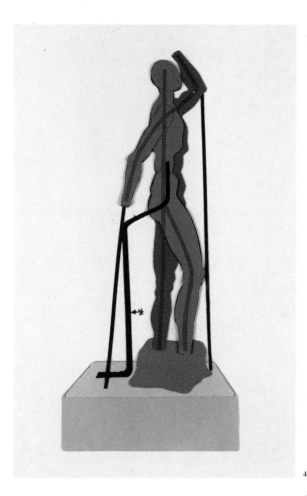

material as a whole. This will weaken the whole piece, making some pieces more fragile than others and taking away the homogeneity and the durability of the clay. In those zones that correspond to where the various segments have been joined, you will almost certainly end up with breaks, cracks and holes, which besides being unfortunate are also impossible to repair. So be very careful to follow this advice: clay is strong and very resistant as long as it is a single unit. If you respect this and turn it to your own use, keeping it as intact as possible, you will get the best from it.

Following are three actual examples of figures. One is lying down, one is standing up and one is sitting. In the photographs you can see clearly some of the different supports that were used.

4. Here you see reproduced a standing figure. As you can see, it is necessary to prepare a metal support for it (indicated by the arrow), which is firmly anchored to the base. This is then inserted into the trunk (from a third to a half of the rod). The legs are resting on a piece of clay which will shrink and pull away from them as it dries. Two rods support the arms.

4

117

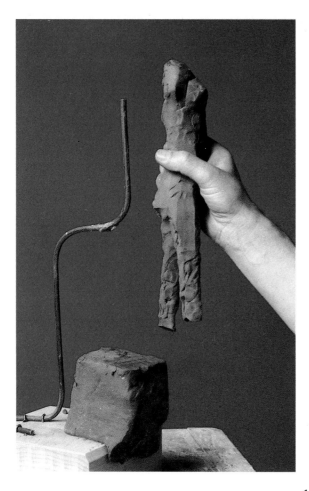 

A practical handbook, by its very nature, is made up of many elements (rules, advice, suggestions, notes and illustrations) which taken as a whole should teach you or at least explain to you in detail how to do whatever it is that it proposes. This can sometimes be as harmful as it is helpful. If it tries to cover too much, for example, it can end up being too general and superficial. For this reason, I want to include a final section to summarise all the rules and illustrations I have given you up to now,

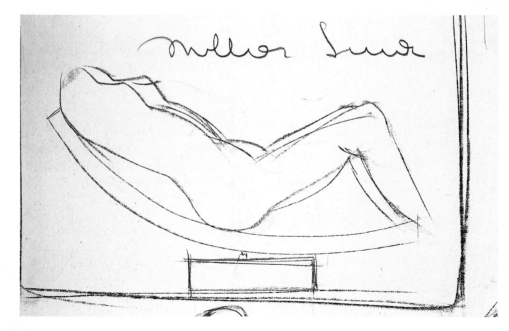

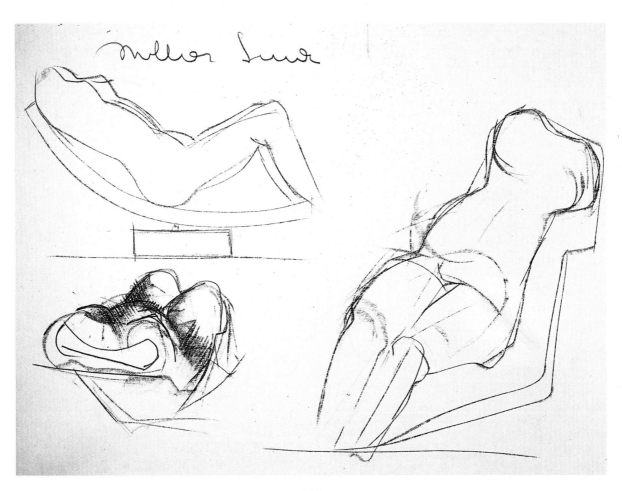

and, as necessity demands it, suggest modifications that you might find necessary in the course of your work (for example, see the note on page 129).

In this last section of illustrations, you will find documented the different phases of work, from the first jottings of an idea to the final stage of firing. This entire "history" is told in one go, without any interruptions or digressions, so as to give you a complete picture of how a work is conceived and made real.

It is a kind of final summing up, a practical synthesis, whose function, or at least so I would like to think, is to bring together ideas and clarify possible doubts that might arise in the course of the earlier chapters. In this last attempt, you will again see graphically and clearly the correct use of the hand as an instrument and the proper employment of the various tools, all of which we have spoken about at length earlier.

There is one last thing that is very important for you to keep in mind. That is, during the whole process of modelling, you must never lose sight of its formal aspect, that is, drawing. At the risk of repeating myself, let me emphasise this again: draw, always draw, as a counterbalance to your work. You should never limit or reduce the dimensions of your ideas because of the technical problems involved in making something. Now and then

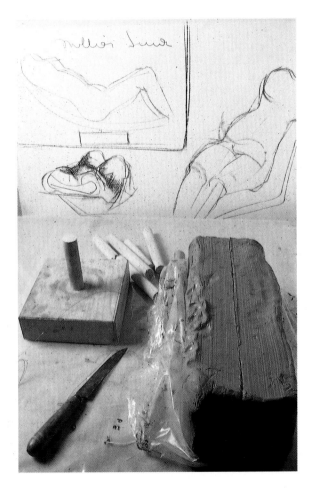

122

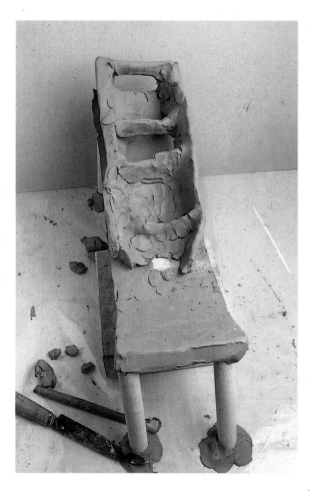

you may encounter some, but do not let them stand in the way of your creativity.

Modelling clay presents innumerable challenges, but patience and planning will allow you to achieve the sculpture you envision.

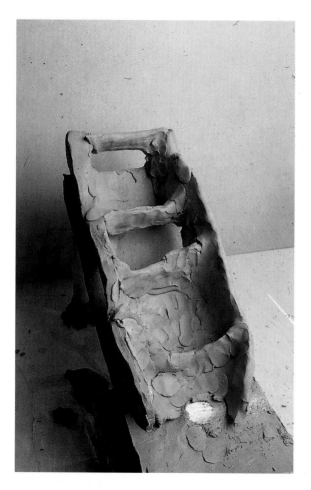

The object shown here seems to me to give a graphic idea of the difficulty that the initial idea can present. As the photographs will demonstrate, even a project that seems nearly impossible can, with a little ingenuity, be executed. From the sketch, I have moved on to show you how to turn it into something concrete, an object which you may find a bit pedestrian and unattractive, but the point is it shows how it can be done and mostly by hand at that. Only one detail makes this last example different from the others I have shown you and that is the fact that it has been made hollow from the beginning. Given the dimensions of this figure, it was not possible to think of making it as one solid piece. The diversity of volume and weight in

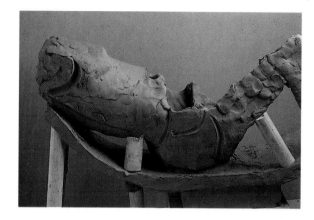

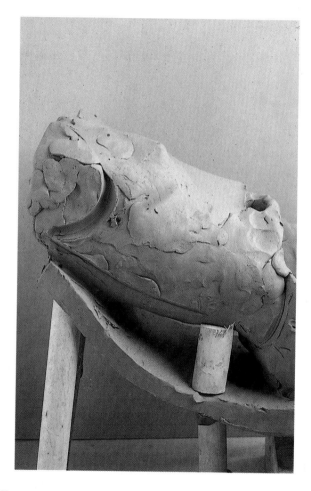

Notice that the initial supports have been completely changed. This is because as the work progressed and the figure grew heavier, the supports were not strong enough to hold it up.

129

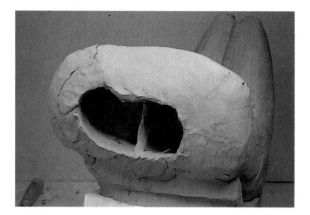 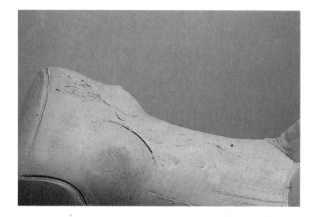

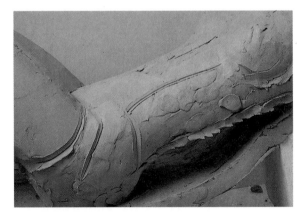 

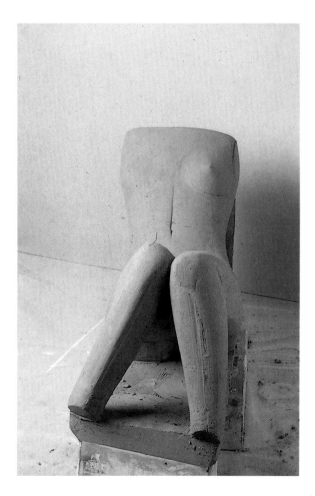

the process of drying would create huge deformities (this is easily understandable if you just look at the difference in volume between the trunk and the legs).

Overall when working on nudes it is never a good idea to remove wedges or windows in order to dig out the clay, the way we did in the earlier bust, because when you go to rejoin them, no matter how carefully they have been removed, there will remain traces of the cut.

For all these reasons, we have worked from the inside out, building from the interior towards the exterior, and paying particular attention to the walls, carefully constructing them all of equal thickness.

The photographs should show you clearly the how and why of the precise arrangement of the underpinnings of support (think of scaffolding in carpentry, used, for example, in constructing a building or holding a boat in place while it is being built).

The only concern you need have in the application of this method is that of creating as much empty space as possible inside the object. Then it is only a matter of working on the modelled form very carefully. Of course, a bit of skill also helps. Finally, let me wish you luck in your work and thank you for having the patience and the indulgence to follow me all the way through to the end.

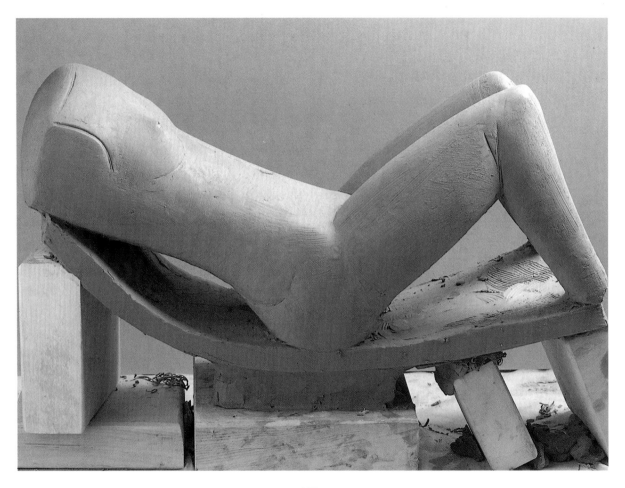

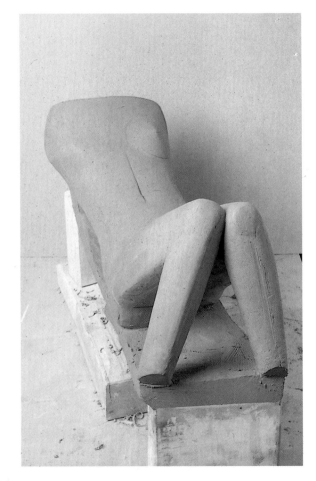

134

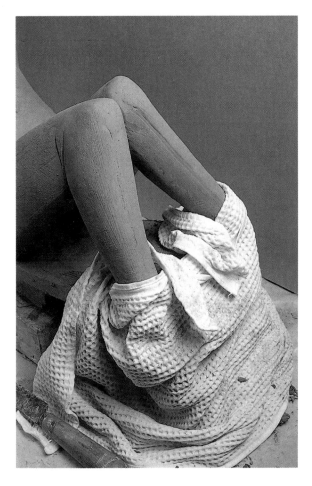

When the sculpture is finished but before you begin the drying process, you should take care to isolate and cover the more delicate parts. They tend to dry more quickly and left unprotected, might dry and become detached from the rest of the sculpture.

135

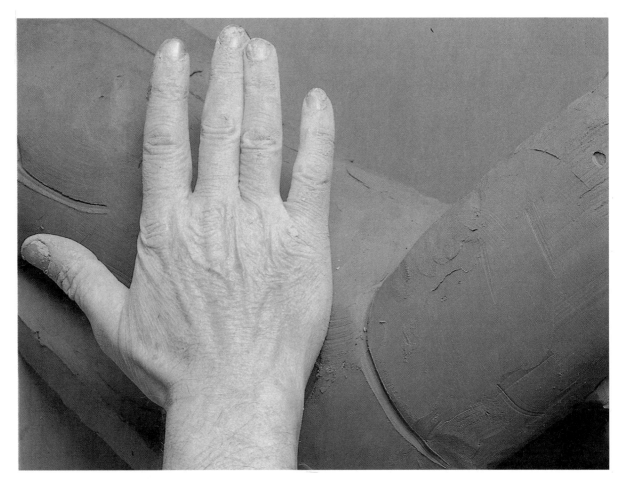

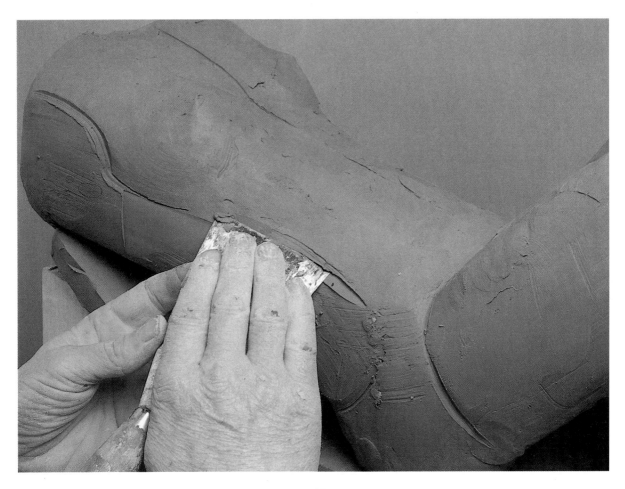

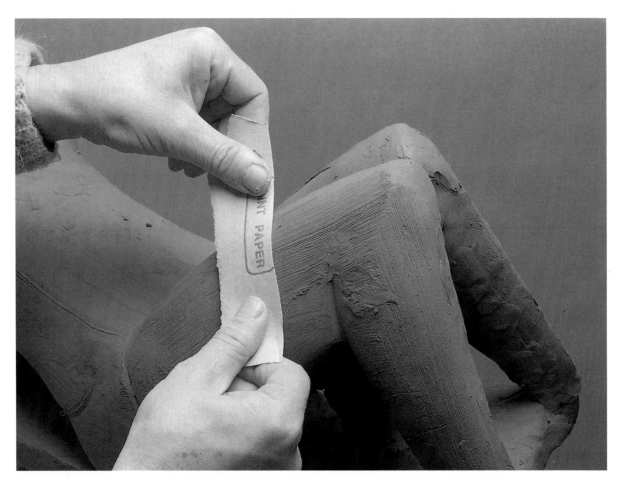

It often happens that when I am looking at a painting, a sculpture or a photograph, or reading a book or listening to music, my curiosity is aroused and I begin to wonder what the author looks like. I do not think this is simply gratuitous curiosity. I think it is something else, something that is not particularly rational. More likely it is instinctive, an attempt perhaps to establish some sort of relationship between an appearance, the physiognomy, the facial expression of the author and his work. Thinking that perhaps others also experience such curiosity, I, whom you have only known up to now as a pair of hands, look like this.

141

Once the process of drying has finished, the sculpture can be taken to the kiln for firing. Don't forget to be very careful with your sculpture when you are transporting it. In the photographs that follow, you can see the progression of events: placing the sculpture in the kiln by an experienced person, the interior of the kiln after firing with the various pieces still carefully arranged on the appropriate shelves, and finally, removing the statue from the kiln when it has cooled.

143

INDEX

Numbers in *italic* refer to illustrations